transcend the
chaos

"Drawing on philosophy, aesthetics, and esotericism, Millar deciphers the rising paradoxes of our era: authority in an age of strangeness, identity in a time of impermanence, and the place of character and consciousness in the unfolding AI epoch. *Transcend the Chaos* is an indispensable and captivating guide for the last Stoics: those who dare to face society's chaos and expectations without losing hope and without losing themselves."

LUA VALENTIA, BRAZILIAN-BORN CHAOS SORCERESS, METAPHYSICAL SCHOLAR, AND VISIONARY AUTHOR

"Let's face it—uncertainty is only going to increase in the future. In this book, Angel tells us how to go beyond the chaos and lead rather than be resigned to change. He shows us how to use a holistic approach that includes personal growth, persuasion, presence, and leadership. I found it fascinating!"

RAM NIDUMOLU, BUSINESS CONSULTANT, ENTREPRENEUR, AND AUTHOR OF *TWO BIRDS IN A TREE*

transcend the chaos

Proven Integral Techniques for Emotional Control, Confidence, and Creativity

Angel Millar

Inner Traditions
Rochester, Vermont

Inner Traditions
One Park Street
Rochester, Vermont 05767
www.InnerTraditions.com

Copyright © 2025 by Angel Millar

All rights reserved. No part of this book may be reproduced or utilized in any form or by any means, electronic or mechanical, including photocopying, recording, or any information storage and retrieval system, without permission in writing from the publisher. No part of this book may be used or reproduced to train artificial intelligence technologies or systems.

Cataloging-in-Publication Data for this title is available from the Library of Congress

ISBN 979-8-88850-243-3 (print)
ISBN 979-8-88850-244-0 (ebook)

Printed and bound in the United States by Lake Book Manufacturing, LLC

10 9 8 7 6 5 4 3 2 1

Text design and layout by Debbie Glogover
This book was typeset in Garamond Premier Pro with Big Caslon CC and Gill Sans MT Pro used as display typefaces

To send correspondence to the author of this book, mail a first-class letter to the author c/o Inner Traditions • Bear & Company, One Park Street, Rochester, VT 05767, and we will forward the communication, or contact the author directly at **angelmillar.com**.

Scan the QR code and save 25% at InnerTraditions.com. Browse over 2,000 titles on spirituality, the occult, ancient mysteries, new science, holistic health, and natural medicine.

For John, my teacher in the art of hypnosis.

Contents

Introduction 1

1
Chaos 4

2
Character and Culture 10

Group Loyalty / Individualism 12 ♦ *Innovation / Tradition 14*
Self-Assertion / Receptivity 18 ♦ *Religious Faith / Secularism 20*
Epicureanism / Asceticism 22 ♦ *Sex / Abstinence 25*
Work / Leisure 27 ♦ *Migration / Settlement 31*
Recognition / Denial of Impermanence 36

3
The Eight Laws of Self-Empowerment 38

Health (or Physical Presence) 39 ♦ *Self-Confidence 40*
Determination 41 ♦ *Will Power 42*
Fearlessness 43 ♦ *Concentration of Thought 44*
Self-Possession 45 ♦ *Perception 48*

4
Eight Daily Power Practices 49
Diet 50 ◆ Physical Training 52 ◆ Sleep 54
Deep Conversation 56 ◆ Deep Reading 57 ◆ Ritual 59
Contemplation 64 ◆ Self-Hypnosis 65

5
The Language of Enchantment 72

6
Self-Talk 84

7
Five Roots of Personal Presence 91
The Face 92 ◆ The Heart 98 ◆ Breath 99
Calm Exterior 100 ◆ Posture 102

8
Chaos Revisited: Strangeness and Authority 105
Authority and Strangeness in Society 108

9
The Six Cs: A Survival Guide for a Time of AI 116
Connection 121 ◆ Creativity 125 ◆ Craft 132 ◆ Culture 138
Character 144 ◆ Consciousness 148

◆ ◆ ◆

Notes 154

Bibliography 167

Index 174

This Book and Your Health

In this book, we speak about diet, exercise, hypnosis, and meditation. You should consult your doctor and seek the advice of a qualified dietician, nutritionist, and/or similar qualified medical professional before significantly changing your diet. Consult your doctor before beginning any strenuous course of exercise or beginning any new type of physical training if you have any preexisting conditions. And get regular medical check-ups. Hypnotic techniques should also only be practiced under the supervision and guidance of a qualified hypnotist or instructor.

Introduction

WE ARE LIVING THROUGH A TIME of unprecedented change. And the speed of change is accelerating. Less than a century ago, it was not uncommon for someone to work for the same corporation their entire adult life and to retire in relative comfort. Over the last few decades alone, however, corporations (and with them entire industries) have collapsed and disappeared. Others, especially in tech, have emerged seemingly out of nowhere, and with them have come new professions, often highly competitive and sometimes quickly oversaturated. Consequently, hard-earned qualifications are at risk of becoming outdated in a surprisingly short amount of time and must be continually updated.

Whether we like it or not, uncertainty and unexpected change are the future. And uncertainty and change affect—and will continue to affect—every area of our lives: relationships, family, how we present ourselves, how we feel about ourselves, the time we have for what is meaningful to us, and even where we will live (or need to live in order to further our career). In numerous ways, the border between work and private life is increasingly eroded. Leaving aside the long hours that some corporations demand, a potential employer might scrutinize your social media accounts before seriously thinking of interviewing you, or you might be expected to act as an unofficial brand ambassador for the company that hires you. Conversely, you need more than qualifications and skills to get on professionally and, increasingly, you will need to cultivate skills of stress management, mindfulness, relationship building, risk-taking, and so on.

Uncertainty. Change. And the Unexpected. These add up to chaos. Yet as we have become more and more specialized in our education and vocation, less able to manage (or thrive under) stress and pressure, less willing to think outside the box, and less capable of exerting influence, we are more vulnerable to chaos than we have probably ever been. Although we will explore how to get on professionally and how to exert influence, this is *not* a book about the economy or professions. It is a blueprint for transforming and transcending chaos.

As you work through its pages, you will learn the secrets of every aspect of personal growth from mindset (chapters 3 and 6) to stress-management, self-development, self-care (chapter 4), persuasion (chapters 5 and 8), presence (chapter 7), and creative thinking and leadership (chapter 9).

To establish a firm foundation for taking action, in the first two chapters we will focus our attention on the nature of society—not as we would like it to be but how it really is. We will look at the role of chaos, chance, and randomness in opportunity. We will see how an advantage can be a disadvantage, and as such, why you should not feel disadvantaged if you have had to struggle. And we will explore the forces that have shaped societies across the globe and that will continue to shape our society and others, noting what we can learn from each. The final chapter constitutes a survival guide for the coming decades. Through it, you will explore what I call "the Six Cs": Connection, Creativity, Craft, Culture, Character, and Consciousness.

At a deep level, things often connect and overlap in interesting and unexpected ways. The lessons of this book draw from a wide range of fields, from marketing to meditation, from hypnotism to the mental aspects of the martial arts, from sales to the creative secrets and business acumen of haute couture fashion. Yet you will find that there are connections between them. And you will discover that the lessons of each are mutually reinforcing. Our approach is holistic, taking into account the whole person.

The path laid out in this book is one of both internal self-development and external application. Feeling more confident, being able to manage and lessen your stress response, and thinking in new and more creative ways are all invaluable in themselves. But in an unpredictable world vulnerable to extreme change, you must take control of yourself and your life and become a leader within it. Leadership does not mean telling other people what to do. It means self-awareness, adaptability, curiosity, creativity, empathy, resilience, and the ability to assess your situation and make a decision about the best way forward. Let's begin by looking at our fast-changing world.

1
Chaos

PHILOSOPHER ZYGMUNT BAUMAN (1925–2017) described our own time as "liquid modernity." Fluids cannot be stopped. They "pass around some obstacles," he said. They spill, drip, flow, and flood. "Fluids do not keep to any shape for long and are constantly ready (and prone) to change it," Bauman also noted.[1] Today, we "go with the flow," are concerned with "market liquidity," and make sure that we have "liquid assets." Even gender is "fluid." Money, identity; everything seems to be in a state of flux. Everything is changing.

Bauman was not the first philosopher to take an interest in liquid. Indeed, we find a similar observation at the very beginning of philosophy. For Thales of Miletus (born ca. 624–620 BCE, died ca. 548–545 BCE), everything was made of water. This seems like a strange idea but Thales might have seen water as the primal substance of life since it can exist in the form of a gas (steam), liquid (water), and solid (ice) depending on temperature.[2] This, in turn, Thales might well have related to the transformation of metal through the metallurgical process of heating, melting, shaping, and cooling, and to the eruption of volcanoes in which molten rock appears as a fiery liquid.[3]

Thales lived roughly a century and a half before Socrates (469–399 BCE), who is often regarded as the father of Western philosophy. Though Socrates wrote nothing himself, through the writings of Plato and Xenophon—who were his disciples in his final years—he has given us the Socratic method of probing a subject through dialogue, or questions and answers, in order to arrive at the truth, or at least as close to the truth as we can get with limited information. This method became a part of classical education and lies at the foundations of such fields as psychoanalysis, therapy, and life coaching.

We must, of course, be able to reason. But rational thinking has definite limits. And believing that the world conforms to rational thought is absurd. Life is chaos. Or as Thales or Bauman might have said, life is liquid. It is always in a state of change: flowing, evaporating, freezing, breaking apart, then flowing again. There are times of calm, but there are also storms. And there are waves, whirlpools, and strong and weak currents.

There is something in Thales's concept of water and Bauman's concept of liquid modernity that is reminiscent of medieval and Renaissance alchemy. Notably, although alchemists attempted to turn base metals into gold through processes of heating, liquefying, and evaporating, alchemy has also sometimes involved the creation of medicines from plants through processes of boiling, simmering, and evaporation. Alchemy has also served as a metaphor for spiritual and psychological awakening. During the twentieth century, early psychoanalyst Carl Jung explored the process of alchemy as a reflection of the psychological process of individuation.

Unsurprisingly perhaps, alchemy is often regarded as the forerunner of modern science. Yet conceptually they opposed each other until very recently. In Europe, the alchemist began with Chaos—or the "watery chaos," as alchemist Simon Forman (1552–1611) described it.[4] Sir Isaac Newton, who practiced alchemy himself, said that "just as all things were created from one Chaos by the design of one God, so in our art [of alchemy] all things . . . are born from this one thing, which is our Chaos."[5] Chaos, if Newton is to be believed, is part of the divine plan. Or to put it another way, it is an inescapable aspect of reality, and as such, acts of discovery, of creativity, and of transformation necessarily involve chaos in some way. In contrast, from its beginning, science rejected the very idea of chaos, or the nonlinear, and assumed instead that natural processes were essentially orderly, or linear.

It was not until the 1960s that the modern study of chaos began. And it began in physics, with the creeping realization that relatively simple mathematical equations, with tiny differences in input, could model systems that appeared disorganized. Described as "sensitive dependence on initial conditions" in relation to weather, this phenomenon became known as the butterfly effect. Accordingly, a minor stirring of the air in one part of the world (e.g., by a butterfly) might lead to changes that ultimately create a storm in another part of the world some time later on.[6]

Over the following decade, a small number of scientists working in different fields (physics, mathematics, biology, and chemistry) began to take chaos seriously.[7] Then in 1976, *Nature* published a "messianic" paper by the theoretical-physicist-turned-biologist Robert M. May in which he observed that the mathematics of "linear systems" (which had been successfully applied to linear problems) had come to dominate the mathematics and physics at the university level.[8] Yet, he observed outside the sciences, nonlinear systems were "surely the rule, not the exception."[9] Chaos needed to be taught if scientists were going to truly be able to understand our "overwhelmingly nonlinear world."[10]

Not only has chaos made a return to the sciences, but the name of Thales has begun to echo in our own time, being used in the names of a number of prominent corporations in the financial, defense, and technology sectors. Perhaps this is not surprising. Aristotle tells us that Thales was once scolded for being poor and told that his philosophy was of no practical use. Thales's philosophy required observing the night sky and the motions of the planets. Through this practice, he had come to believe that the next olive crop would be unusually abundant; it was still winter at the time. Thales paid deposits on all of the olive presses in Miletus, where he lived, and in Chios, which was some distance away. Since they were not in demand and no one else bid on them, he was able to hire them cheaply. When it came time to harvest the olives, there was, as Thales had predicted, an abundant crop. The olive presses were now in high demand and he was able to hire them out, making a substantial profit. He did this not because he wanted the money but to show that, through their knowledge, philosophers can become wealthy.[11]

Yet, Thales's ability to predict harvests is not the only point of connection to the financial world today. In *Trading Thalesians: What the Ancient World Can Teach Us about Trading Today*, Saeed Amen tells us that "Thales' notion of water . . . can actually be closely related to the concept of risk [in today's financial markets]."[12] While Western societies tend to conceive of the wealthiest 1 percent (and therefore the other 99 percent) as essentially fixed, even here there is constant flux: a staggering 70 percent of wealthy families lose their wealth by the second generation and 90 percent lose it by the third generation.[13] As some people move out of this demographic, others of course move in, though their families will be no more immune to the cycle of familial financial boom-and-bust than those they replaced.

Of course, you might feel that those born into wealth are still at an advantage, but 70 percent of the children of wealthy parents are not. Two-thirds of the remaining families will lose their wealth with their grandchildren. If the grandparents could make themselves wealthy, it is plausible that most of their offspring could at least have increased their wealth if they had been born into equally humble circumstances, rather than lose it during their lifetime. The children of wealthy parents do, of course, sometimes make more wealth. But adverse circumstances often instill outsiders with the drive and ambition to succeed despite the odds.

Although a small percentage of families will keep their money generationally or lose it far more slowly over many more generations, for most, in a world of chaos and constant change and new challenges, being born into wealth is a disadvantage. The children of the self-made wealthy learn to spend rather than to create. And what comes easily, goes easily. Still, you might envy their easy ride through life and their ability to buy whatever they want. You might think of them as free of the worries you have experienced. They will not know what it means to struggle to pay the rent. But spoiled and entitled, such people often feel—and perhaps are—inadequate and unloved.

We have friends to the degree that we have character and gravitas. These qualities are carved out in facing challenges, in aspiring, pushing through discomfort, cultivating endurance and fortitude, and in overcoming our struggles and accomplishing goals in our lives. Of course, we all have acquaintances as well. These are people that we like but that do not know our struggles and accomplishments and we do not know theirs. The grown-up children of the self-made wealthy usually attract only acquaintances—mere hangers-on who want to help them spend their inheritance. Of course, the children of the wealthy will often use their money to get what they want, including sexual or romantic partners. But deep down, they know that their attractiveness and power is entirely derived from the character, gravitas, and work of others. They, themselves, are empty.

Let's return to chaos. Psychologist Albert Bandura observed that most models of human development regard childhood experiences as laying the foundation for the course of the individual's life. And while an individual's character, interests, and abilities are likely to strongly influence their life in certain regards such as career, the "branching power" of random, impactful encounters makes an individual's life difficult to predict.[14]

Sometimes, the branching power (or we might say "the butterfly effect") of a random encounter can be entirely negative. Bandura mentions the case of Diana Oughton, a sensitive, sheltered individual from an affluent family who, by a chance encounter, was set on a course that would lead her to join the terrorist Weathermen organization. She was killed when a Weathermen bomb went off accidentally.[15] Nevertheless, unexpected encounters can also lead to enormous changes in life trajectory that are overwhelmingly positive and that can ultimately shape society to a large degree. Steve Jobs and Steve Wozniak, the founders of

Apple, met when Jobs was out walking with a friend, Bill Fernandez; Wozniak was also a friend of Fernandez. And Sergey Brin and Larry Page, the founders of Google, first met when Brin was giving a tour of Stanford University to new students. Page happened to be one of them.[16]

As Bandura notes, influence in human society operates—or at least tends to operate—reciprocally rather than unidirectionally. The degree to which you will be able to capitalize on chaos in the form of "fortuitous opportunities" and resist entanglements that might lead to disastrous consequences is dependent on the development of your "personal resources" and "personal agency." These include the acquisition of competencies (knowledge and skill in particular fields), self-agency, and self-direction.[17] Or to put it more simply, it is our competence and our character that determines our ability to navigate, defend ourselves against, and capitalize on the chaos inherent in life. We will explore these throughout this book.

2
Character and Culture

IN THEIR *LESSONS OF HISTORY*, Will and Ariel Durant tell us that there are six traits of the human being, each of which has its opposite.[1] These traits, which the Durants say are significant factors in the shaping of history, are (1) action/sleep, (2) fight/flight, (3) acquisition/avoidance, (4) association/privacy, (5) mating/refusal, and (6) parental care/filial dependence.

It is peculiar, perhaps, that the Durants did not include religious belief in their list of characteristics. Human beings have relinquished sex and sworn themselves to chastity because of their religious convictions. They have flogged themselves until bloody. They have seen visions and created great works of art to commemorate saints or to express the sacred. And they have fought wars and conquered "unbelievers" in the name of religion.

We might make another adjustment to their list, subsuming parental care/filial dependency under the greater category of association/privacy. The family unit has been indispensable to society but the nuclear family is relatively new. Previously, the extended family was the norm and often these functioned almost as small tribes. Again, families with many children whose parents could not, as such, give much time to any one of them were typical and younger children were often partially raised by older siblings. Among the upper classes, children were often sent to boarding school and saw their parents infrequently. In ancient

Sparta, boys were removed from their families at twelve years of age.

We must add another category: migration/settlement. Human beings have found themselves called—almost religiously—to scale the tallest and most forbidding mountains and to go to the Arctic, even though, inhospitable to human life, neither of these could be made into permanent settlements. Armies have traveled halfway across the world to conquer territories. Human beings tamed horses and camels and turned them into modes of transport. Then we invented other means to transport us farther and faster across the land and still others to take us across the oceans, through the air, and into space. On the individual level though, the migration/domesticity dichotomy may determine much about our future in a fast-changing world in which travel and migration are integral to it. As an individual, we might perhaps move abroad to study, immigrate for work, marry, or join family members. Or we might spend our entire lives in the same town that we were born into. But even so, the community around us will likely change and we might find ourselves in a place that feels as strange as if we had left.

Lastly, we should take note of both the recognition and the denial of our mortality and how these shape individuals and cultures alike.

With these adjustments and minor changes in verbiage to suit our purposes, we might settle on the following nine characteristics:

1. Group Loyalty / Individualism
2. Innovation / Tradition
3. Aggression / Receptivity
4. Religious Faith / Secularism
5. Epicureanism / Asceticism
6. Sex / Abstinence
7. Work / Leisure
8. Migration / Settlement
9. Recognition / Denial of Impermanence

Let's consider each of these in turn.

GROUP LOYALTY / INDIVIDUALISM

There is an Arabic proverb: "My brother and I against my cousin and my cousin and I against the stranger."[2] Traditionally, a person owed their loyalty to their family, tribe, and—later—their nation-state. The Arabic term for "loyalty," "group consciousness," or "social cohesion" is *asabiyyah* and North African historian Ibn Khaldun* (1332–1406, born in Tunis) tells us that it is asabiyyah that provides the incentive for a community to develop from primitive conditions to civilization—or from a family to a tribe and eventually to a nation-state.

Unifying the community, asabiyyah prevents internal strife and external attacks, enabling it to grow and develop. According to Ibn Khaldun, while blood ties are enough to unite the tribe in its earlier stages, after statehood has been achieved the asabiyyah of lineage will be replaced by an asabiyyah of reason, and instead of blood ties there will be a collective commitment to the dynasty and its religion.[3]

However, in the West, both Christianity—the dominant religion in the West over the last millennia—and belief in the nation-state have radically declined. Instead, we have come to believe in a global society, a "global village," or multicultural societies composed of different nationalities and cultures. Along with these have emerged the belief in international law, open borders, and mass migration. Consequently, within the borders of Western nation-states, group loyalty is actively opposed if that loyalty is based on traditional "in-group" ties, such as the nation-state itself, or on the nation's traditional customs, religion, or familial structure.

Group loyalty, or prejudice, has not disappeared of course. Instead, pushed down in one area of life or society, it reemerges full force elsewhere with new divisions and with "out-groups" being transformed into "in-groups" and vice versa. Today in the United States, discrimination

---

*Wali al-Din ʿAbd al-Rahman ibn Muhammad ibn Muhammad ibn Abi Bakr Muhammad ibn al-Hasan Ibn Khaldun.

against people of a different political party affiliation is more common and far more acceptable than discrimination on the basis of religion.[4] Such is the unceasing churn of history.

As social psychologist Henri Tajfel (1919–1982) showed during the 1970s, whether we like it or not, human beings always categorize themselves into groups and discriminate in favor of those in their group (the in-group). Conducting a series of studies during the early 1970s, Tajfel and his colleagues assigned participants to categories that were as meaningless and arbitrary as possible. Yet the participants still exhibited group loyalty to members of their own arbitrary and meaningless group; for example, awarding higher points to members of the in-group than those outside of it.[5]

Those who believe that they are not prejudiced and that they are open-minded and do not discriminate, in fact, discriminate against other groups as much as everyone else.[6] Simply, their prejudices might be rationalized away or regarded as moral and might even be applauded by influential segments of society such as the media or politicians. Especially in a cosmopolitan city such as London or New York, someone who would be shocked and appalled by the sentiment encapsulated in "my cousin and I against the stranger" might nevertheless embrace its inversion—the stranger and I against my cousin—creating a new group loyalty.

Increasingly in our time, group loyalty is leveled against the most creative, innovative, and dynamic members of society. To create, quite simply, is to court condemnation. Perhaps this is inevitable. Creators, innovators, and disruptors of all types upset the status quo, not only at the very top of society but perhaps, more problematically, in the middle, among the ordinary people—or what we might call the new "moral majority." This group has played by the rules and now finds that those rules are under threat by new innovations, new technology, and ways of doing things. Yet creative thinking and the ability to think differently and to innovate is precisely what enables a civilization to survive. Ironically, group identity is integral to individual identity.

Takeaway

An individual's sense of self is largely based on who they identify with regardless of whether this is their closest neighbor or a complete stranger. Of course, you must endeavor to cultivate friendships with people you respect and where there is the opportunity for mutual respect and support.

However, also think carefully about who you identify with outside of friendships and family, and identify yourself with those who mold circumstances to their advantage rather than being molded, and disadvantaged, by them.

In relation to other people, to motivate the individual to act in the way you want, invoke the values and signifiers of the group that they identify with and remind them of their membership in that group.

INNOVATION/TRADITION

Let's draw from the five-factor model of personality used in the realm of psychology, which describes the traits of extraversion, neuroticism, agreeableness, conscientiousness, and openness to experience. Innovation suggests high openness to experience (i.e., to new experiences) and tradition suggests low openness to experience. Societies tend to value one or other of these, of course. The West tends to value innovation, change, novelty, excitement, gimmicks, and so on. Even though they may be innovative in such areas as technology, at the present time countries such as Russia and Iran tend to value tradition, especially their religious traditions.

An extremely innovative society and an extremely traditional society will both have their advantages and disadvantages as well as social benefits and problems. In traditional societies, families tend to be larger and family members lend support to each other. In innovative societies, families are small (and in the West, ever decreasing in size), which creates greater financial insecurity and greater reliance on the government for help. In traditional societies, too, work is typically more stable, with people remaining in a single job for many years or even for their entire lives. In innovative societies, as we have mentioned, entire industries can collapse, jobs are unstable, and an individual might need to change professions over the course of a lifetime.

As with too much tradition, too much innovation can be boring, producing endless novelty that is a mere spectacle and that lacks any sense of depth, meaning, or purpose. Extremely innovative societies can also be hostile to those who want to live more traditional lives, whether inside or outside of their borders.

At its most extreme, as "progress" becomes a belief verging on a religious faith rather than a creative act, the innovative society becomes as intolerant as—if not more intolerant than—the traditional society. It will spend its energy on making sure everyone conforms to the political beliefs du jour and will unleash modern-day witch hunts on nonbelievers.

Since it can be interpreted in different ways, eventually creativity itself may fall under suspicion. There is always the possibility of interpreting a creative product or work of art as being out of step with or opposed to the current ideology or latest cause. The "free love," free speech, and freedom of conscience that enthused the creative elite and that was inseparable from their society's most innovative stage is replaced by an emphasis on morals and rule following. Creators and thinkers begin to censor themselves. No ideas and no facts can be debated and those that contradict the narrative are regarded as unspeakable. The uncreative become the loudest voices. Posing a threat to its long-term survival, the innovative society starts to become anti-creative and even begins to mirror the most dogmatic of traditional societies.

While there will be those who resist and go against the demands of their society, whether it is innovative or traditional, the individual is often a microcosm of their society. The traditional society generally produces individuals who are closed off to the world, to ideas, and to other possibilities. The innovative society produces atomized individuals whose opinions change with the latest media reports, whose family ties and friendships are tenuous, whose knowledge of history is virtually nonexistent (so that they are not able to learn its lessons) and whose lifestyle is based on consumption, pleasure, and the avoidance of pain and unpleasantness.

The mean between the extremes of innovation and tradition is creativity. And over the last few decades, creativity has declined in the United States and doubtlessly elsewhere in the Western world. We tend to associate creativity with the arts. And certainly, it is integral to art, design, music, and similar pursuits, but an individual who is highly creative is more likely to become an inventor, entrepreneur, diplomat, doctor, author, or college president.[7] Creativity is fundamentally about problem-solving and, as such, is the engine of civilization. Creative individuals adopt the spirit and attitude of past creators and build upon tradition while pushing into new creative territory.

On a societal level, creativity requires that the populace is enthused by the best of history and tradition while being willing to entertain new ideas and possibilities. On an individual level, especially in our unstable and fast-changing world, we must choose some skills or arts (business, technology, fine art, medicine, literature, martial arts, etc.) and master them to the best of our ability. Being highly knowledgeable or skilled in at least one area enables us to understand other skills or areas of knowledge with greater ease. Indeed, innovation often comes from combining seemingly separate areas of expertise.

Innovators must also be willing to take manageable risks. First then, you must know what you can and cannot afford to lose if the gamble does not pay off. Things rarely work out the first time and so some loss is almost certainly unavoidable. But in defeat there are invaluable lessons to learn. Reaching any significant, long-term goal in life will require treading a path of trial and error, and this will mean determining manageable risks from unmanageable ones.

Understanding your limits right now, and how far beyond them you can push, will require honest self-reflection and a little humility. Here, then, we should think briefly about confidence and arrogance. There may be different ways to define these but we can think about them this way: Confident people ask questions. Arrogant people have an answer for everything.

Confident people are interested in things that they do not know about. They are curious and inquisitive. They are able to ask questions and show that they do not know anything about a particular subject because they are confident that they know a lot about some other area. Thus they ask questions not as an inferior, but in the spirit of exchange. If you have a question for them, they will answer to the best of their ability.

Confident people are able to exchange ideas, knowledge, and perspectives with others. In contrast, an arrogant person will always steer any conversation away from things they do not know about to something that they do know about. Or they will talk over other people to prevent the conversation being taken where they do not want it to go. Quite simply, they want to be seen as clever or knowledgeable, even though their knowledge is limited, one-sided, and unbalanced at best.

Creativity requires curiosity and inquisitiveness. And it requires the willingness to take manageable risks, the ability to assess our strengths and weaknesses, confidence in what we know, and willingness to learn more.

On a societal level, however, if innovation gives way to dogmatism and confidence turns into arrogance that society will not be able to survive major shocks or challenges. To survive, societies often depend on outliers—creative individuals who can withstand scrutiny and condemnation, or high-IQ immigrants (see the "Migration/Settlement" section below) who are either unofficially exempted from some of the cultural norms of society or who do not care about the criticism of a society that is not theirs.

Takeaway

(1) Cultivate curiosity. The world is complex and sometimes contradictory. Ask questions so that you can understand the world a little better.

(2) Appreciate the best of traditional culture but learn to think and act in original ways. (3) Reflect honestly on your skills and your weaknesses, and understand what risks you can and cannot afford to take in pursuit of your goals. (4) Exchange knowledge and information with people at a similar level in your field and in other fields.

SELF-ASSERTION / RECEPTIVITY

If the five-factor model of psychology was our guide here, we might speak of extraversion and agreeableness instead of self-assertion and receptivity. But these are not exactly the same. On the side of receptivity we have ancient notions of hospitality, which is as integral to the Bedouins of today as it was to ancient European tribes a millennia ago. Yet here, though the stranger will be welcomed into the family home and fed, he must play his part; he must not, for example, leer at the women of the house. Both the host and guest play by ancient rules.

Again on the side of receptivity, we can speak about openness to aspects of other cultures. It should not be denied that every culture and civilization has developed organically, according to its own logic or rather according to its own unifying myths. But every civilization has absorbed and reinterpreted aspects of other cultures that it has come in contact with. To give only one example, although it originated in Mesopotamia, pottery decorated in blue and white became popular in the Islamic *ummah*, China, continental Europe, and Great Britain, though the decoration varied from culture to culture.

Institutions of self-assertion and receptivity have been established in every civilization: the former being those of war, sport, politics, and festivals such as Saturnalia (characterized by drunkenness, sex, pranks, and games); and the latter being those of mysticism, monasticism, education (dispassionately exploring ideas from all different perspectives), and scientific inquiry.

Yet we also find the aggressive and the receptive being unified in a higher ideal: the warrior-monk or the warrior-poet or warrior-mystic.

Hence the Roman emperor, general, and philosopher Marcus Aurelius; the berserker and poet Egill Skallagrimsson; the warrior and Muslim mystic 'Ali ibn Talib; the samurai warrior and painter Miyamoto Musashi; and the religious mystic and warrior Joan of Arc.

You may notice that the idealized warrior brings us back to creativity. This is a poet, a painter, a person of culture, and a thinker. An army general must think more like an artist, by thinking nonrationally and doing the unexpected. Always doing what is rational in war makes an army easy to predict and easy to defeat.

The mean between self-assertion and receptivity is self-development or, we might even say, self-ennoblement. It is becoming who we should be, beyond limited expectations and cliches—embodying our own nature and refining it, and not apologizing for who we are or what we desire.

Most people are content to conform though they want to be seen as special. And they want to do what they have always done. If they like sports and fighting, they will stick with sports and fighting. If they like art and music, they will stick with art and music. The majority see themselves as a type: intelligent, compassionate, tough, effeminate, artistic, rationalistic, and so on, and as such, to interact with the world they are forced to rely on intellectualism, emotion, inappropriate aggressiveness, flamboyance, and so on. They conflate their limitations and quirks with personality and believe that these give them an identity that distinguishes them from the groups of people that they have merged themselves into.

Takeaway

Be clear about who you are and what you want out of life. Develop appropriate self-assertion and appropriate receptivity. In regard to the latter, acknowledge your limits and weak spots and learn from people who can help you improve in those areas. See things from different perspectives and seek out new ideas and possibilities. In regard to appropriate self-assertion, focus and put energy into pursuing your goals. Cut out time-wasting activities and people. Reach out to those who can help.

RELIGIOUS FAITH / SECULARISM

"The first effect of not believing in God is to believe in anything," wrote the Belgian playwright Emile Cammaerts.[8] In the West, of course, atheists focus their criticisms against Christianity, not Hinduism, Jainism, or New Age religions. They will often point out that Christians do not believe in gods such as Zeus and, on this basis, will argue that in this sense we are all atheists (disbelieving in many gods) or that atheists only disbelieve in one more god than the monotheist.

While this may be amusing, belief itself doesn't just disappear. Rather, it is transferred onto other things or systems. The communist dictatorship of North Korea has all kinds of official myths about its ruling family. According to one, at the time of Kim Jong Il's death, an impenetrable sheet of ice inside Mount Paektu cracked open and the sky above glowed red. In another, his son, Kim Jong Un, was supposedly "born of heaven."[9]

Of course, most secular beliefs are less obviously a mimicry of religious myth, but they can be held every bit as fanatically. In our own time, every few years or less, political ideas and campaigns come into vogue that cannot be questioned. There is always a backlash, of course, but on both sides we find the same pressure to conform. Unsurprisingly perhaps, a 2022 *New York Times* and Siena College poll found that 46 percent of respondents felt "less free to talk about politics" than they did a decade previously.[10]

Yet peculiarly, in the West as political ideas and campaigns change they often express the exact opposite of what was previously endorsed by the same believers. The actual beliefs themselves may be of secondary or even minor consideration. More important than the details is some kind of faith that the individual can conform to, can use to carve out some semblance of an identity, and as such, can use to orient themselves in a chaotic and unpredictable world. Not only do we exist within an environment of ever-changing beliefs and political positions but also of consumer fashions, fads, and product updates. Nothing is lasting or stable. All that we can say for certain about the future is that we will not believe tomorrow what we believe today.

Both religion and secularism can lead to intolerance, fanaticism, and irrationalism. Yet religion has also created much beauty in the form of the architecture of the cathedrals, mosques, and temples; painting and sculpture; music; ritual; and annual holidays. Moreover, all of these were created to express the belief in something beyond our mundane lives and to remind us of the vastness of time and space, the miracle of creation or of life, our relationship to ancestors, the meaning and purpose of our lives, and our relationship, in one way or another, to that mysterious Intelligence that we, in the West, tend to call God.

Atheists see the religious claim that "God moves in mysterious ways" as simply an excuse to not look at any situation logically. And no doubt it can be misused in exactly this way. But one of the problems of the modern individual is precisely that we have an answer for everything. Such answers are not our own, of course. Rather, they are absorbed, usually unthinkingly and unflinchingly, through the media.

We all have deeply held beliefs, of course, although we often simply think of our beliefs as "the truth." Whether in religion, politics, or other areas of life, illogical beliefs are often the ones we hold onto most fanatically, for such beliefs cannot sustain rational probing and, as such, demand blind obedience. They are also the beliefs that give us a sense of identity.

Frequently, people hold onto self-limiting beliefs because this makes them feel more intelligent or more moral than other people. They can tell themselves that they haven't "sold out" or are unlike those successful people who must have gotten to the top through corruption or connections. After a painful breakup, someone might tell themselves that they will never find love again while pushing away suitable romantic partners. A person who prides themself on being rational might cut themself off from the things that naturally give life meaning: love, nature, art, and so on.

You might know the Zen koan about the Zen master Nan-in.

An opinionated university professor visited to Nan-in one day, wanting learn about the teachings of Zen. Nan-in began pouring tea for his guest and kept pouring it until the cup was overflowing with tea. The professor shouted for the Zen master to stop, saying, "no more will go in." Nan-in then likened the overfull cup to the professor's mind.

In the West, the average individual is like that professor. No more will go in. We have an answer for everything even though what we really need are deep questions of our own. We need to contemplate and, if we want to rediscover joy, meaning, and purpose in life, then perhaps more than anything, we need to recognize that some things cannot be explained away and that we must rediscover a sense of Mystery, a sense of awe, and an appreciation for beauty and simplicity. Most things that give us meaning are not rational and cannot be calculated and evaluated through charts and statistics: music, sex, attraction, love, beauty, nature, and so on.

Takeaway

Change someone's beliefs and you will change their actions and, thus, their life trajectory. Change your own beliefs and you will change your own life trajectory. Since the strongest beliefs are often impervious to rational argument, you must fire the imagination. Everything can be interpreted in different ways; in a trial, the defense and prosecution will argue that the same evidence has opposite meanings. Change the language you use to describe your beliefs and your beliefs will change.

EPICUREANISM/ASCETICISM

Our contemporary term *epicurean*, referring to the love of luxury and indulgence in sensual pleasure, derives from the ancient Greek philosopher Epicurus (341–270 BCE). But the philosopher lived much more simply than our term suggests. Born in Samos, he later traveled to Athens and went into military service. Then he purchased a house and established a small community there, which came to be known as Ho Kepos ("the Garden"). Epicurus and his followers lived plainly, drinking mostly water, except for a modest ration of wine each day, and eating bread. Epicurus taught his followers to avoid politics. He was also suspicious of sexual relations and even marriage. Instead, he placed great emphasis on friendship.[11]

We, however, are more concerned with the contemporary meaning of *epicurean* and its opposite. According to *Forbes*, the average American is about fifty times wealthier than the average English person was in 1600 CE (or living in communist China in 1978). In such subsistence economies, greater wealth means more food, which translates into a greater likelihood of survival for children.[12] In contrast, increasingly across the globe we live in societies that are focused on consumerism. Especially in the cities where people are atomized, individuals seek distraction in the form of alcohol, junk food, entertainment, and sexual novelty.

We cannot really call this "decadence" in the sense that it was used a century ago or less, since, though the term hinted at cultural decay even then,* *decadence* also usually implied excessive richness and the indulgence of the senses permitted only to a small and often highly creative elite. The "decadents" were revolutionary artists, writers, and thinkers and their wealthy patrons. To join such circles wasn't easy. An individual had to possess a certain style, had to have an understanding of culture, an ability to speak with wit and intelligence, and had to contribute something financially or artistically.

Rather like food, which over time has become increasingly processed and made with artificial flavors, the beliefs and material culture of the elite eventually filters down to the rest of society, albeit in lower quality and imitation forms; hence the emulation of high-end design by high street shops and the market for fake designer goods (especially luxury bags).

No matter who we are, if we don't look too closely at the quality, virtually everything is available to us at any time and requires little or

---

*From French *décadence* and Latin *decadentia*, meaning "decay."

no effort to acquire. The one thing we are denied is the one thing that we might desire the most, however: anticipation.

Because we can get almost anything we want, whenever we want it, we never look forward to anything. Seasonal celebrations were once major events, planned for and looked forward to weeks or months in advance. There was something magical, mysterious, and memorable about them. Today we can indulge our senses as if every day is Saturnalia. Notably, most British supermarkets now sell the traditional Easter treat of hot cross buns (sweet bread rolls made with spices and dried fruit and decorated with a cross) throughout the entire year so eating them at Easter is no longer special and no longer something to look forward to.[13] In dating, too, in the back of our minds we know that there is always going to be someone better than our current date within easy access via a dating app. Yet easy availability and instant gratification make our indulgences habitual, ordinary, shallow, boring, and even addictive.

When excess becomes ordinary, we can either take a step back and reevaluate or double down. In general, Western societies have decided on the latter course. In the fine arts, for example, an artwork is more likely to be sold for its shock value than its artistic merit. But nothing really moves us because we have seen it all before. In terms of cultural impact, movies have taken the place of paintings. But here too, we find story being sacrificed to special effects. The result is the same. What is supposed to be exciting is boring.

The opposite of self-indulgence is asceticism—going without luxury or convenience and living simply. Of course, ascetic communities still exist here and there today, including in the United States, such as the Quakers. But we need to rediscover what the Greeks have called *philokalia*, from *philia*, "love," and *kalos*, "good." In our own time, there is a growing interest in natural aesthetics and ingredients and a growing recognition that the natural, the healthy, the aesthetically appealing, and the good are often linked.

For the ancient Greeks and for many later cultures, the beautiful was inseparable from "the good." Whether embodied in a cathedral painting, the tile work of a mosque, or the reliefs of a Hindu temple, it is expressed most especially through proportion and harmony. The same idea has been applied to the body. As Wang Keping has noted, the ancient Greeks "would resort to regular gymnastic training in order to build up fair and masculine bodies. At the same time, they would develop themselves into *kaloi k'agathoi* as the synthesis of physical beauty and good character."[14]

Takeaway

Whatever is easily accessible is forgettable. Cheap imitations are everywhere. Whether we are speaking of a person in regard to a relationship, or a consumer object, whatever is of high value is comparatively rare. Although they are opposites, one thing that the decadent and the ascetic have in common is a preference for quality over quantity. Whether in romantic relationships or business, seduction means not being too accessible, creating anticipation, and exhibiting value.

We often think in terms of balance when it comes to relationships, food, and other aspects of our lifestyle. But we're not always clear about what balance actually means—beyond, perhaps, cheating on our diet or acting in a way that is incongruous with our values. Before the modern era, money in the form of gold and silver coins would be weighed on a pair of scales. Why? Simple. Forgers would create fake coins using cheap metal coated with gold or silver.

Balance, then, is inherently about two things: (1) value and (2) what is real or authentic. Evaluate what gives your life value and what is authentic to who you are. Keep the gold and get rid of the lead weight that is pulling you down.

SEX/ABSTINENCE

In 1937, popular author Napoleon Hill suggested that most people who "succeed in an outstanding way"[15] do not do so before they are in their forties or fifties. The reason, he claimed, is that individuals have a "tendency to dissipate their energies through overindulgence in physical expression of the emotion of sex."[16] Or to put it more plainly, they are too preoccupied with sex. However, he says, because sexual lust is the most "impelling" of all desires, if we are able to harness and transmute this desire into other actions, it might raise us "to the status of a genius."[17]

Certainly, success can come late in life. For example, Charles Darwin was fifty years old when his landmark book *On the Origin of Species by Means of Natural Selection* was published, as was Bram Stoker when *Dracula* was published. But the age in which genius is expressed in a particular field depends largely on when the individual began their studies in that field—the later the start, the older the individual will be when they master the subject.

The relationship between sex and genius is complicated. There have, of course, been highly sexually active geniuses and, at least in the arts, sexual activity and creative activity is often obviously linked. Painter and sculptor Pablo Picasso lost his virginity in the brothels of Barcelona at thirteen and would later form a habit of going from one woman to the next, leaving a trail of tears and heartbreak along the way. Most notably, as Picasso aged, his sexual partners did not, with the last three all being in their twenties when the relationships began. The last of these, Jacqueline Roque, was twenty-seven when her relationship with Picasso began; he was seventy-two. To some extent, to Picasso these younger women were his muses and he would portray them in his work, though sometimes unflatteringly.

Nevertheless, as Isaac D'Israeli (1766–1848, author and father of nineteenth-century British prime minister Benjamin Disraeli) observed, many artists and men of genius prefer to remain celibate, unmarried, and childless in order to devote themselves to their life's work.[18] This is a decision only for the few, however, and cannot become a significant trend without disastrous results. During the final years of the Roman Empire, "birth control and a disinclination to marriage became widespread," notes Vladimir Gregorievitch Simkhovitch in *Rome's Fall*

Reconsidered. A similar phenomenon occurred in ancient Greece as well. People grew greedy and idle. Marriage became rarer and when people did marry they had only "one or two children" so that their offspring could enjoy their inheritance, Simkhovitch tells us. Consequently, the cities began to empty.[19] Quite simply, most people must reproduce or their civilization, nation, or tribe will collapse.

However, if most people must procreate for the civilization to be kept alive—equally, the few must devote themselves to the creation of what we might broadly describe as "culture" (e.g., the fine arts, the sciences, and philosophy). Thus, while some creators may entangle themselves in sexual liaisons and others may be happily or unhappily married, D'Israeli's observation was correct: celibacy is overrepresented among geniuses.[20] In a study of British geniuses published in 1926, Havelock Ellis showed that, excluding priests, nearly one in five were celibate. Another study by H. G. McCurdy, published in 1960, found that 55 percent of elite historical figures never married.[21]

Takeaway

Avoid relationships that drain your time and emotions. Do not give in to demands for constant attention. You have your own life and your own goals. Personal growth and success in life requires energy, commitment, work, and time to think, act, and adapt. Choose your friends and lovers wisely.

WORK/LEISURE

"In fact, it is by the use of leisure that we may judge the characteristics of a people,"[22] wrote industrialist Henry Ford. But what is the "use" of leisure? What is it for? Is it merely to enable the individual time to rest sufficiently in order to begin work again the next day or the next week? Is it meant to enable them to forget work briefly, thus making it more tolerable? Is leisure something confined only to those who work? Or as Ford implies, does—or should—leisure serve a higher purpose?

According to Thorstein Veblen (1857–1929), a theorist of the "leisure class" and a critic of capitalism, upper-class society uses leisure to distinguish itself from—and as such, as a weapon against—the working class. Leisure, he says, "considered as an employment, is closely allied in kind with the life of exploit, and the achievements which characterize a life of leisure . . . have much in common with the trophies of exploit." These achievements include, he says, the "quasi-scholarly" (much like his own writing, perhaps), the "quasi-artistic," and "a knowledge of processes and incidents which do not conduce directly to the furtherance of human life," including music, dress, furniture, games, sports, "correct spelling," and studying "dead languages."[23]

Almost anything that is not drudgery and that might elevate the human mind or spirit Veblen regards as nothing more than a hand grenade, lobbed by an aristocrat at a defenseless worker. It was, we must acknowledge, Veblen who introduced the idea of "conspicuous consumption," still used today, but his critique is otherwise out of date. Leisure is no longer a symbol of status, if it ever was in the sense that Veblen conceived it. Rather, status today is demonstrated by its opposite, particularly in the United States: long hours of "busyness and overwork."[24] As such, Veblen's critique cannot help us to understand what leisure is for.

Perhaps Henry Ford gets us closer. He declared that "Man needs leisure to think, and the world needs thinkers." Yet, again, the German Catholic philosopher Josef Pieper (1904–1997), reminds us that theologian and philosopher Thomas Aquinas (ca. 1225–1274) believed that it is for the good of society that some men should dedicate themselves to the "'useless' life of contemplation."[25] This sentiment sharply contrasts Veblen's critique in which what is good is implicitly what is useful. But a life of only useful things (the hospital, the car mechanic's toolbox, the mousepad, the washing machine) is a life of utter dreariness. It is a life in which each act of each individual is continually engaged in some act of utility that leads merely to some other act of utility. It is a life not only without art, music, or poetry unless they can be harnessed to propaganda, but also without watching the sunset or walking along the beach and without love, true friendship, or joie de vivre.

Leisure, Pieper tells us, is nothing less than "one of the foundations of Western culture."[26] However, by leisure he does not mean merely taking a break from work, living for the weekend, relaxing on the beach during a vacation, or stupefying the senses through mindless consumption of alcohol and entertainment. Nor does he mean conspicuous consumption. Rather, for Pieper, leisure is "an attitude of mind" and "a condition of the soul." It is "an attitude of non-activity, of inward calm, of silence," he says. And it is that silence that we require if we are to apprehend "reality."[27] Pieper reminds us, too, that during the medieval period, "there was a distinction between the understanding as *ratio* and the understanding as *intellectus*."[28]

Ratio is "examination," "logical thought," and "drawing conclusions." It is active. It is the way of understanding, exalted and taken to an unbalanced extreme by Ayn Rand, who proclaimed that "Happiness is only possible to a rational man, the man who desires nothing but rational goals, seeks nothing but rational values and finds his joy in nothing but rational actions."[29] As we have said about usefulness, this must exclude virtually everything human beings find meaningful, from sex to music. Rand fetishizes the producer just as she fetishizes the rational. But "rational production" is the mantra of the Soviet factory, not the genius—who is not a producer but rather, an inspired figure.

In contrast to ratio, intellectus is passive. It is contemplation, intuition, and apprehending the real, for example, by contemplating a landscape and being moved—and uplifted—by it. Pieper's comprehension of leisure is, of course, religious. Proposing that leisure is rooted in religious "celebration" or "festival,"[30] he reminds us that certain days and times were first set aside in antiquity for the worship of the gods.[31] But its purpose is to enable us to contemplate and to become who we truly are.[32]

Even leaving religion or spirituality aside, leisure enables us to think or, more accurately as Pieper says, to contemplate. As Ford notes, intelligence gives us "the ability to receive," but merely listening to remember some nugget of wisdom, "merely wondering" or worrying "is not thinking." Instead, vaguely reflecting the medieval division of ratio and intellectus, Ford tells us, "Thinking is creative or it is analytical."[33] Thinking requires time. But inspiration and breakthroughs in thinking also require relaxation.

Genius requires relaxation—to loosen, open up, to become less tense and less formal. It requires us to step back and to let go of our attempts to force an answer by going through the same mental drills (ratio) and to allow inspiration to come to us. It is nonrational or supranational; we will explore this later in relation to hypnosis. Of course, used wisely, leisure enables us to read, think, to expand our mental horizons, to exercise our mind and body, practice an art, and so on. But in a time in which we are constantly consuming (including consuming information and ideas), we need to allow things to gestate and to emerge out of our own consciousness—to have, in other words, our own beliefs.

Enabling us to step outside the world of work, production, and ratio, leisure serves the ultimate purpose of reconnecting us to who we truly are, awakening in us our creative genius, and enabling us—occasionally at least—to become inspired. The creative individual, the leader, and the genius especially require intellectus, not mere rationality and usefulness. And they require it because—unlike the ordinary person who is outer-directed, wanting social status and worldly success—the genius is "inner-directed," "inner-driven," and "inner-motivated."[34]

Takeaway

We can get lost in the endless flow of information and ideas. Instead of filling every minute with distractions, consuming information that you have consumed in only slightly different forms already, and busy work, take time to relax and to contemplate or *think*. Once they have been sought in rational problem-solving, answers to problems often emerge seemingly out of nowhere in moments of relaxation when you aren't working.

MIGRATION/SETTLEMENT

We tend to think of most countries as being demographically stable across time. Yet history tells us that migrations and even "great migrations" have remained a constant factor in world history. From 3500 to 1500 BCE, Proto-Indo-European-speaking peoples (probably descended from the Yamnaya, living on the Pontic-Caspian steppes)[35] spread outward across vast swaths of land into Europe and Asia. From these groups of nomads descend such languages as English, German, French, Spanish, Greek, Celtic, Polish, Russian, Armenian, Urdu, Hindi, and Farsi.[36]

The seafaring Phoenicians of the ninth to seventh centuries BCE reached both Western Europe and West Africa.[37] Alexander the Great (356–323 BCE) created an empire that spread from Greece to the Indus Valley in India. And during the fifth century CE, Angle, Saxon, and Jute tribes migrated to Great Britain, laying the groundwork for the emergence of the English people.[38] During the seventh and early eighth centuries, after the rise of Islam, the Arab peoples began a massive territorial expansion, conquering the Persian empire, Egypt, Libya, Palestine, Syria, eventually creating an empire that spread from the Indus Valley to Spain.[39]

Over the centuries, highly intelligent and creative foreigners and international travelers have shaped our world. Indeed, long periods of travel abroad are almost the norm among such figures. Here are named only a tiny fraction of them:

> **Galen** (129–216 CE). A Greek physician born in Anatolia (now Bergama, Turkey), Galen studied in Smyrna (modern İzmir, Turkey) and later in Alexandria, Egypt, where he remained for more than a decade. He later moved to Rome and traveled with emperors Lucius Verus and Marcus Aurelius to northern Italy on a military campaign. Galen's writings exerted a strong influence on medicine in Western Europe from the medieval period all the way through to the mid-seventeenth century and had a similarly

lasting impression in the Byzantine Empire and the Muslim Middle East.⁴⁰

Benjamin Franklin (1706–1790). A diplomat, inventor, printer, publisher, and author, Franklin lived in America, Great Britain, and France.

Jamal ad-Din al-Afghani (1838–1897). A political theorist, journalist, and agitator against the Western colonial powers in the Middle East, al-Afghani traveled widely throughout his life, settling in Afghanistan, Istanbul, Cairo, India, and Iran.

Friedrich Nietzsche (1844–1900). Born in Rocken, Saxony, Prussia (Germany), Nietzsche became a professor of classical philology at the University of Basel, Switzerland, in 1869, and later lived on the French Riviera and in Italy. He died in Weimar, Thuringian States, Germany.⁴¹ Telling us that "God is dead . . . And we have killed him,"⁴² Nietzsche was perhaps the first philosopher to recognize that after approximately a millennium in the West, Christianity had lost its grip on the European imagination and could no longer unify or guide Europe or the modern world as a whole. His writings have exerted a strong influence on philosophers, thinkers, and artists since his lifetime.

Albert Einstein (1879–1955). A recipient of the Nobel Prize for Physics (1921), Einstein is known for developing the special and general theories of relativity. Born in Ulm, Württemberg, Germany, he finished his schooling and then studied at university in Switzerland. He renounced his German citizenship and was, for a time, stateless until being granted Swiss citizenship in 1901. He later traveled widely, speaking at international conferences, and died in Princeton, New Jersey.⁴³

Pablo Picasso (1881–1973). Born in Málaga, Spain, and living in Barcelona with his family, he moved to Paris in his twenties. Becoming one of the most influential artists of the twentieth century, Picasso worked in painting, sculpture, and ceramics, constantly developing and reinventing his oeuvre.⁴⁴

Mahatma Gandhi (1869–1948). Born Mohandas Karamchand Gandhi in Porbandar, India, he moved to London, England, in 1888 to study law and later spent over two decades in South Africa. Afterward, he returned to India, becoming a leader of the Indian anti-colonial movement and used nonviolent protests to effectively push out the British.[45] In contrast to the popular image of Gandhi dressed only in a white loin cloth, in London he appeared as a model English barrister, wearing a three-piece suit and white shirt with starched collars. There, on one occasion, he was asked by two Theosophists if he could help them read the Bhagavad Gita, the main text of Vedanta Hinduism. Founded by Mme. Blavatsky, a Russian immigrant to the United States, the Theosophical Society was and still is involved in the study of mysticism, drawing on a wide array of the world's religious and spiritual traditions, especially ancient Egyptian and Hinduism. Gandhi confessed that he had never read the Bhagavad Gita but agreed to read it with the two Theosophists. The meeting turned out to be fortuitous. Gandhi was surprised by the wisdom of the sacred book and began thinking of it as a guide for his conduct. In 1917, Blavatsky's successor Annie Besant gave Mohandas Gandhi the title that he has become known by: *Mahatma* ("great soul").[46]

According to the Pew Research Center, as of 2022, over 280 million people are international immigrants (3.6 percent of the world's population). In other words, migration remains a major force in shaping the world in our own time and will doubtlessly remain so in the foreseeable future.[47] However, the United States has more foreign-born persons than any other country by a wide margin (over 50 million), followed by Germany (15.8 million), Saudi Arabia (13.5 million), Russia (11.6 million), the United Kingdom (9.4 million), United Arab Emirates (8.7 million), France (8.5 million), Canada (8 million), Australia (7.7 million), and Spain (6.8 million).

Immigrants to the United States* have traditionally been considerably more entrepreneurial than American-born citizens,[48] and the children of immigrant fathers have out-earned the children of U.S.-born men.[49] Most strikingly, in 2010, more than 40 percent of Fortune 500 companies were founded by immigrants or the children of inmigrants,[50] among them Elon Musk (PayPal, Tesla), Sergey Brin (Google co-founder),[51] Pierre Omidyar (eBay), and Osman Kibar (biotech firm Samumed).[52]

Unsurprisingly then, the success of immigrants to the United States has long been a cause of speculation among public thinkers. Of course, immigrants tend to move to places with strong job growth while many native-born Americans remain in their hometowns even when the local economy is stagnant or declining. However, when members of the latter group move to places of strong job growth, they earn as much as the children of immigrants.[54] Like the individual who moves within their home country, the immigrant clearly has a different psychology to individuals who remain where they were born as the economic environment stagnates or worsens.

Immigrants face psychological pressures in response to being separated from family and practical challenges such as a lack of famil-

---

*Immigration is undoubtedly a complex subject. Unfortunately, studies generally do not distinguish between persons who originally entered specifically for higher education, employment with a U.S. company, other legal immigrants seeking asylum or entering for family reunification, or "unauthorized immigrants," all of whom face different challenges and have very different levels of education. Foreigners applying to work in the United States (i.e., for the H-1B visa) must have a bachelor's degree or higher or, less commonly, specialized training and experience considered to be the equivalent of a U.S. bachelor's degree. See U.S. Citizenship and Immigration Service, "H-1B Specialty Occupations, DOD Cooperative Research and Development Project Workers, and Fashion Models." By comparison, in 2016, 44 percent of unauthorized immigrant adults between the ages 25 and 64 did not have a high school diploma (down 3 percent since 2007).[53] The likelihood of an immigrant to the United States falling below 200 percent of the poverty line is determined by different factors, "not the least of which are education levels and length of time in the United States." See Majority Staff of the Committee on Ways and Means, 2004 Green Book, "Background Material and Data on the Programs within the Jurisdiction of the Committee on Ways and Means," J-8, available on the GovInfo website.

iarity with social norms in regard to personal and professional relationships that others do not. Yet, living abroad also seems to facilitate experiences and engender personal qualities that become an advantage. After studying 3,000 executives, 500 founders of innovative companies or inventors of novel products, and 25 innovative entrepreneurs, Jeffrey H. Dyer, Hal Gregersen, and Clayton M. Christensen found that living overseas increases the likelihood that an individual will innovate. Moreover, if a manager has even one international assignment before becoming CEO, they discovered, the company they lead will perform roughly 7 percent stronger in the market than companies headed by a CEO with no international experience.[55]

Let's look at two important qualities of being a successful outsider.

Living with Risk

Human beings are naturally risk averse. We prefer familiarity to change. Often individuals, organizations, and cultures will stick with familiar habits and ways of thinking even when, in a continually changing world, they become detrimental to survival. The foreigner, in contrast, lives in an unfamiliar environment to the one in which their character, assumptions about life, and habits were forged.

Often, too, the foreigner has either no support network or a very small network of support in comparison to native-born individuals. Most obviously, they usually have no family or, at least for many years, long-term friends in the country they have moved to. This is especially the case if the foreigner has moved abroad on the basis of exceptional skill or accomplishments and thus is not part of a wave of migration from a specific country or region, which will be made up of lower-skilled individuals.

Today, usually reliant on a visa apparatus that can reject visa renewals for any reason, the longer such a person lives abroad, the more the highly skilled or exceptional individual will be invested in their new life and more estranged from their old life and old society. In other words, the foreigner is forced to accept risk, to live permanently outside their comfort zone, and to view failure as simply not an option.

Cultural Comparison and Contrasting

Confronted by differences in history, culture, customs, and worldview, intelligent individuals who live abroad will inevitably contemplate, compare, and contrast their home country and their adopted country. An intelligent outsider will, as such, be able to recognize the strengths, weaknesses, and blind spots of both, and will be able to embrace and appreciate the best aspects and reject the worst aspects of both. Through the process of contemplating, comparing, and contrasting, they will be able to see what is missing or what opportunities exist in different areas of life. The foreigner must think independently, creatively, and differently. They must appreciate the best of what is and, at the same time, see possibilities for improvements.

Drive, willingness to accept risk, appreciation, the ability to think outside the box, and an ability to see blind spots, weaknesses, possibilities, and opportunities is a powerful set of inner qualities. Combined with a deep knowledge of a particular field or an exceptional level of skill, an individual might become almost unstoppable.

Takeaway

Experience different cultures and live in a different city or country if you are able, especially if your hometown is in a state of economic stagnation or decline. Acknowledge what is good in each but be aware of blind spots, weaknesses, and opportunities in both. If you can't travel, widen your circle of friends and learn from people of different backgrounds. Moreover, get used to evaluating risks and taking the risks that are manageable.

RECOGNITION / DENIAL OF IMPERMANENCE

During the medieval period, skulls were sometimes painted on the reverse of portraits, as well as in some still-life paintings full of other objects that represented the sensuality and transient nature of life. In contemplating one's own mortality, the individual was able to turn toward the eternal (God, heaven, etc.) and away from the material world and its impermanence and trials (e.g., higher infant mortality, disease, and limited medicines).

As the West has become more secular over the last few centuries, especially over the last few decades, our earlier religious beliefs have been transposed onto politics and economics. Hence our belief in immortality has been replaced by a belief in infinite economic growth and the hope that we will reach heaven in the afterlife has turned into the hope that, through government intervention, we will create a heaven on earth.

Busts follow booms. Bear markets follow bull markets. Yet our conviction that we are always progressing shelters us, emotionally and psychologically, from the reality that we live in chaos, and that everything in a world of chaos is unstable and impermanent. By refusing to reflect on the nature of change, our own mortality, and that time to accomplish our goals is short, we feel that we do not need to adapt or that we need to remain the same as we were twenty or thirty years ago; an example is the aging celebrity pop singer who insists on dressing and acting as if they were in their early twenties.

Strangely for our time, Steve Jobs said that he asked himself each morning if he was doing what he would want to be doing if it was his last day on earth. If the answer was "no" for too long, he knew that he would have to change something.[56] To recognize and to be mindful that our time is limited is to begin to understand that we were not meant to waste our time or our life but, instead, must actively seek out how to live.

Takeaway

Recognize that time is short and that things are always changing. Reevaluate and update your self-presentation as time passes. Endeavor to grow, learn, become more skillful in all areas of life, adapt as necessary, and through experience, become more certain of who you are. The time to act is now.

3
The Eight Laws of Self-Empowerment

FROM OVERWORKING TO OVEREATING, from junk food to junk media, our society is badly out of balance—flailing around, seesawing one way then another. All that it holds dear one year, one month, or one week, society trashes the next. And those who are feted by a long line of celebrity sycophants are soon denounced. Nothing appears stable or permanent. There are few, if any, examples of the kind of person that we want to be. And there appears to be little possibility for self-actualization in such a world. And yet, as the Buddhists have always known, the lotus grows out of the mud, toward the light.

Your light is your own vision and highest ideals, and those who exemplify them in whole, or more probably in part, whom you can learn from. But to begin to forge yourself—mind, body, and spirit—in accord with that vision, you must establish a foundation or base (your base level, in physical training terminology) in the midst of this world of chaos and uncertainty.

At the beginning of the twentieth century, Dr. William Wesley Cook spoke of the qualities of the successful hypnotist. As you will realize, these qualities are also essential to the authentic leader: physical presence, self-confidence, determination, willpower, fearlessness, concentration of thought, self-possession, and perception.

Here, we are going to explore these qualities. And we are going to look at their role in self-empowerment, self-development, and success in the world.

HEALTH (OR PHYSICAL PRESENCE)

Although Cook tells us that physical health is essential to the hypnotist, he hints at something more. "A strong and vigorous physique exerts a great influence upon those of less favored bodily condition," says Cook. In other words, our physical appearance and presence can, and should, create a sense of authority. You might have witnessed a beautiful woman walking into a room and the men sitting up straighter all of a sudden. Certainly at some point, you have found yourself wishing that you looked more like someone else that you regard as more attractive or wishing that you possessed the charm of some especially charismatic individual that you have met. You might even have begun to imitate them in certain ways.

Physical presence requires good health. An attractive physique is helpful. So is wearing clothing that suits you and that either reflects some aspect of your personality or your authority in a particular situation. This might be a tailored suit in a professional situation; it might be a biker jacket in another. It might be a long black dress or a pantsuit. It depends on the context.

When it comes to making the right impression (or trying to), people often think of clothing in terms of symbolism rather than aesthetics. A man will buy a ready-to-wear suit that is a couple of sizes too large or wear a black shirt with a white tie, while a woman might wear an ill-fitting red dress. The suit might be supposed to signify success or power. The black shirt and white tie is supposed to signal that the wearer is someone who knows what's cool. And the red dress might be supposed to signify a fiery, passionate, or daring disposition. Ultimately, to those in the know at least, the ill-fitting symbolic outfit fails to deliver. Clothing should draw our attention to the wearer, not to the clothing itself.

Good posture, a sense of confidence, and a sense of being relaxed but "in the moment" are also essential when it comes to personal presence. In later chapters, we will look at health, posture, and other aspects of personal presence. Focus on the situation at hand or on the person you are conversing with; people rarely have anyone truly and deeply listening to them and so listening can, in itself, be highly seductive.

SELF-CONFIDENCE

According to Cook, self-confidence is of primary importance to the hypnotist. And of course, self-confidence is essential to the process of actualizing your true self and to becoming a creator or a leader of any kind. Yet your self-confidence must "be backed by manifest ability," he says. "One must actually possess power before he is able to exercise it."[1] Too many people today are convinced that if they "believe" something will happen, then it will happen. In most cases, it won't.

Self-belief and self-confidence cannot be based on a fantasy. It must grow as your abilities are cultivated and sharpened, as your successes stack up, and as you contemplate and learn from defeats and setbacks. Becoming more experienced and knowledgeable means that you will be more able to recognize your own strengths and weaknesses and to work on the latter to improve yourself in different areas.

Self-confidence also means boundaries. When our achievements begin to stack up, we are often asked—or pressured—to take on too much work or too much responsibility. This could be within a corporation or within a relationship or voluntary organization. Or sometimes, friends or a romantic partner might pressure us to be socializing all the time when we have decided to dedicate most of our time to completing a particular task or project. At a certain point, you will need to start saying "no." To do your best for others, you need to do your best for yourself first.

We instinctively know what the self-confident person looks like: they not only appear confident but also healthy, happy, friendly (we probably envision them smiling), calm, kind, helpful, and willing and eager to listen to others. Such people make us feel good about ourselves even as we want to be more like them. We are instinctively drawn to such persons.

Setting boundaries and focusing on what you need to do does not mean cutting other people off. Indeed, you must cultivate relationships. Simply, it means getting the most value out of your time. When you are working, focus on work. When you are socializing, focus on your friends. When you are on a date, focus on your partner.

DETERMINATION

For Cook, the defining quality of determination is the ability to keep going after experiencing failure. Although you must constantly evaluate your progress and recognize when it is time to adapt or change course, in themselves failures are not reasons to quit. Everyone fails at some point and the masters in any field failed numerous, perhaps countless, times on their journey toward mastery. Failures must be analyzed and lessons must be learned from them. Painful though such experiences may be, they are opportunities for growth. Those who do not become expert hypnotists, says Cook, "are too ready to 'give up.'" The same applies in all other fields.

When Angela Duckworth, the author of *Grit: The Power of Passion and Perseverance*, studied why West Point cadets dropped out, she discovered that those who stayed the course weren't always the most qualified. Some lagged significantly behind others in terms of ability but they persisted, learned from their mistakes, and with persistence, got better and sometimes even overtook other cadets. The ability to overcome failure—or being "resilient and hardworking"—was one of two factors. The second factor was vision. "[T]hey knew in a very, very deep way what it was they wanted," says Duckworth. "They not only had determination, they had *direction*."[2]

What separates the warrior from the wannabe is the ability to keep going. Accept failure now. It will happen. It is part of the journey. It is necessary for growth. Get used to it. Don't make a big deal out of it. Don't blame others. Analyze each failure. Simply figure out how you can adapt and grow to give yourself a better chance of success in the future.

WILL POWER

Typically today, we associate "willpower" with determination and the ability to push through obstacles in life. What Cook meant by "will power," however, was the ability to command others. "It is this power which raises a volunteer from the ranks to the generalship of an army," he says. And this phenomenon is found in individuals in all walks of life. "Even among boys at play," says Cook, "there will be some one who will control the others by his will power, and his fellows will obey him without hesitation."[3]

Leaders have will power, but with the corrupt or self-serving "leader"—this power is backed up primarily by the threat of violence, usually to be committed by other people. The authentic leader's will power is backed up by the respect the listener has for them, and this respect is typically based on the leader's experience, character, ability to understand how certain courses of action are likely to play out, and ability to remain level-headed in times of great pressure.

Of primary importance, however, is your ability to command yourself. Often, we sabotage our plans and good intentions by falling back into bad habits. An individual might want to lose excess body fat but, after a few days of eating a healthy diet, finds themselves giving in to an old craving for junk food.

Another obstacle can be friends and social events. Friends will often make excuses for us, partly because they do not want to upset us, partly because they might fear confronting us, and partly because they might not want to work on their own shortcomings, preferring us to remain who and where we are. Even in romantic relationships, one partner might encourage some particular bad habit such as snacking or drinking alcohol every night, partly because they want their partner to be happy; partly as an excuse not to clean up their own act; and sometimes, perhaps unconsciously, partly as a way of controlling the other individual.

Learn to command yourself. To command yourself you must know yourself. Understand, right now, that big promises usually mean big excuses. Growth in any area of life is usually incremental, occurring over a long period—usually years or more. Start small if you need to. If you haven't worked out in a few years and plan to train at home rather than at a gym, start with a few minutes a night. If you've never meditated before, start with five minutes each morning. Or if you're planning to launch a new business but have been unmotivated for weeks, months, or longer, just promise yourself that you'll do ten or twenty minutes each morning or evening.

Be clear about when you're going to start—not what time, as things can get shifted around, but whether it's right after you wake up, after you shower, after you get home at night, and so on. Most of the time, once you've been going for five minutes or so, you will want to spend more than the minimum time you allotted. Getting started is harder than keeping going. Make starting as practically and psychologically effortless as possible.

FEARLESSNESS

Cook defines *fearlessness* as "the willingness to dare without hesitation." However, this is open to misunderstanding and to encouraging foolish behavior. The ancient Greek philosopher Aristotle noted that things are "destroyed by defect and excess." The individual who is too frightened to stand their ground against anything is a coward. At the other extreme, one acts foolishly if they rush toward every threat, unprepared. The point of balance between cowardice and rashness is courage.[4] We need to cultivate courage.

Generally, confidence and courage grow slowly as we move forward in life, taking one step at a time—facing down one manageable risk after another—gaining experience, developing skills, acquiring knowledge, learning how to adapt to changing circumstances, experiencing successes as well as failures that we can reflect on and learn from, and consequently, becoming better at predicting how a particular course of action will play out.

CONCENTRATION OF THOUGHT

To concentrate on a single thought or idea, or to visualize a certain object or objective, is not easy. Very soon the mind wanders off, pursuing some new train of thought, and—swept up in the imagination—the individual is usually unaware that this is occurring. Only moments later do they realize that they've been thinking of something other than what was intended. Suppose we decide to visualize a ball of light and to think of nothing else whatsoever. Soon we think to ourself "this is easy," congratulating ourself on the successful ability to think only of the ball, not realizing that now we are thinking these other, congratulatory, thoughts.

What applies to mental concentration applies to life. Most people allow themselves to be distracted from their goal. An individual might set out to pursue one objective but will get sidetracked, sometimes by a new goal—especially if they have made a habit of jumping from one thing to the next—and will sometimes be distracted by the promise of a fleeting pleasure that emerges on the horizon.

The individual might, for example, have decided to get physically stronger but soon, instead of working out, will begin hanging out with friends, drinking alcohol, getting drunk, polluting the body they wanted to perfect. And—feeling tired and nauseous the next day—they will be unable to work out as planned. Or one might have decided to learn a new skill but, finding some distraction, give up upon reaching the first plateau. Or one might have decided to launch a business, but get sidetracked by a romantic relationship, or vice versa.

SELF-POSSESSION

For Cook, self-possession simply meant not being angered, and not becoming upset at or feeling defeated by circumstances beyond our control.[5] If something goes wrong in our work or life, we have to remain composed and we have to respond intelligently, using whatever resources we have—time, the ability to work hard, contacts, support, and so on—to stay or get back on track.

However, many people today prefer to live their lives in a state of dispossession of their true nature. Or to put it another way, rather than cultivating their vision of what they can and should become (if they even have such a vision), they prefer to live according to some fantasy, seeking pleasure or validation without putting in the work. Such individuals leap from one venture to the next, one hobby to the next, and of course, from one sexual relationship to the next, never committing to anything or anyone. Enthusiastic at first, they quickly see the flaws in whatever they pursue but never see the flaws, or real potential, in themselves. Their constant chasing after the momentary emotional high is a way of avoiding looking at themselves.

Self-possession requires self-awareness. And that requires the ability to look dispassionately at your own strengths and weaknesses, to cultivate what is healthy and to fix or eliminate what is unhealthy in you. This process of self-examination and self-correction must be practiced constantly.

Unfortunately, many people think that merely believing and visualizing will make their dreams "manifest" in reality. This notion is mostly associated with the "positive thinking" movement, also sometimes referred to as the New Thought movement or mind metaphysics. There is much value in the positive thinking movement, which has influenced contemporary spirituality, business, and sports, as well as many other areas of the modern world for the better, especially in the United States. While some people overestimate their knowledge and ability in different areas of life, probably far more people underestimate their potential.

Many people tell themselves that they are incapable of achieving what they would like to achieve. For the latter group, positive thinking can be a big help. But positive thinking must always be followed up with consistent, positive action.

Most people find excuses not to act. An individual can put off getting fit, eating a healthy diet, quitting an unwanted habit, launching a business, or learning a new skill for another week, month, year, decade, or—just as easily—for an entire lifetime. In most cases, such individuals simply lack vision and commitment. They are easily distracted, insecure, or unsure of themselves, and they are content enough with their lives to not risk going out into the unknown and the uncertain.

No matter how intellectual or spiritual they may be, those who rightly believe in the power of the mind but wrongly will not follow through with action are another type of consumer. As we have already seen, human beings need belief, and in a world in which the religions seem either corrupt, dangerously fanatical, or wholly compromised, perhaps the belief in belief itself is understandable.

But if such individuals are correct that belief itself causes changes to occur in the world—and the stronger and the more sincere the belief, the more likely our desire is to manifest in the physical world—how is it possible for them, or us, to experience surprise or shock? We only experience these emotions when we truly believe that one thing will happen but it does not, or when something entirely unexpected, unimaginable, or unthinkable occurs instead. And the more we believe that something will occur, the greater the surprise or shock we experience. All of us have experienced this.

While our beliefs can be wrong, we all know that the belief that we can succeed is essential for motivation. However, as we have already noted, self-possessed, accomplished individuals *believe* they can succeed through hard work, dedication, the willingness to learn and improve, intelligence, and self-sacrifice—putting off pleasure today for accomplishment tomorrow. And their belief grows as they witness themselves achieving small victories on their chosen path. They do not believe that belief in itself will manifest their desires for them.

There are, of course, two possibilities when we believe strongly that something will occur: either it will or it will not. We have all experienced both countless times. There is a strong element of chaos—chance or apparent randomness—in the world and in life. And this is as it must be.

It is only because of the underlying chaos of life that we experience chance encounters, are presented with new opportunities, discover things we had never thought of, find ourselves in new places, or find ourselves faced with new challenges that force us to grow. And it is only this underlying chaos that enables us to turn the tide of culture, belief, and emotion to our advantage and—inspiring others by example—to the advantage of those who are either like us or who want to be like us. This underlying chaos is freedom and it can only be molded with courage, creativity, and intelligence.

We have spoken quite practically about self-empowerment, but we must acknowledge there is also a metaphysical, mystical, even magical element to it. If we marry our vision and our belief to action, providence often appears to aid us. As if by chance, opportunities, guidance, or much-needed information appears. Sometimes things seem to move very quickly and effortlessly.

At other times, however, our beliefs about the future are proven false, often right down to very small and specific details. While this phenomenon is not acknowledged in the positive thinking world, it can seem just as mysterious and providential as periods when everything goes right and things fall into place as if it was destined. And very often, later on we see that it was being proven wrong that forced us to open our minds and it was those periods of struggle that forced us to grow, to develop ourselves, and to push ourselves far out of our comfort zones. Indeed, while we all wish for good fortune, great persons—people of resilience, courage, and daring—are often forged, early on, in bad luck and undesirable circumstances while comfort, security, and good luck conspire to create weak individuals.

Malleable, chaos is shaped by those actions that we take toward realizing our vision, as well as the actions of other people, whether complementary or competing. It is the raw energy that underlies and energizes all events, large and small. You must learn to perceive it and to manipulate and mold it as a sculptor molds clay or chisels stone to create art—their true self-expression.

PERCEPTION

Cook limits his discussion of perception to the observation of a person in a hypnosis session. However, you must develop the ability to perceive not only the subtle drives, reflexes, behaviors, and motivations of other people, but also your own unconscious drives, reflexes, behaviors, and responses.

As human beings, we are often remarkably ignorant of our own desires and motivations, and remarkably adept at creating a self-image that is as saintly as it is untrue. If you can confront your own attempts to deceive yourself—by remaining stuck in various areas of your life or behavior and blaming others—not only will you be able to steer your course toward your vision and toward your true nature, you will have a greater understanding of other people.

To aid you in this, further on we will explore language, posture, and even the unconscious use of your facial muscles. This will give you insights into your true self and into the false image that you present to the world and to your own conscious mind.

4
Eight Daily Power Practices

IN THIS CHAPTER, we are going to look at eight practices for cultivating well-being, a powerful mindset, and creativity. The first three of these are diet, physical training, and sleep. While essential to maintaining physical health, these also affect our mood and, as such, thoughts and decisions—or mindset. And that is what we are ultimately concerned with both in this chapter and throughout this book.

Information about what we should and should not eat is always changing, and of course, we are each different and have different dietary restrictions and requirements. Moreover, our bodies change over time. Food that was suitable for us in one stage of life might not be suitable for us in another.

Take your health seriously: Seek the advice of your doctor before changing your diet, get the help of a qualified dietician or nutritionist, and get an allergy test to test for food allergies and intolerances. In regard to exercise, get a check-up from your doctor before beginning and find a reputable trainer. Don't go it alone.

The remaining five practices are partially concerned with mental, and even what we might broadly call "spiritual," well-being, though you do not have to be religious or have a specific spiritual practice to incorporate these into your daily routine. Four of the five will also help you to develop your mind, imagination, intuition, and as such, your creative potential.

Together, the eight practices are (1) diet, (2) physical training, (3) sleep, (4) deep conversation, (5) deep reading, (6) ritual, (7) contemplation, and (8) self-hypnosis.

DIET

Every part of our body is controlled by our brain and nerves: our organs, glands, muscles, and reproductive system—everything. When Dr. David Friedman told this to a group of medical students he was met with a simple, if unusual, question. If the brain and nerves control everything in the body, what controls the brain and the nerves? His answer was simple: food.[1] And yet, it is relatively rare to encounter an individual who prioritizes nutrition. Instead, we often eat or drink habitually, out of boredom, or because we are stressed, upset, or emotionally feel low.

Nevertheless, in recent years there has been a growing awareness of the link between food and mood and even between food and more serious psychological issues, hence the development of "nutritional psychiatry."

Between 2012 and 2015, a number of volunteers were recruited for the SMILEs (Supporting the Modification of Lifestyle in Lowered Emotional States) study led by Felice Jacka, founder and president of the International Society for Nutritional Psychiatry Research (ISNPR) and director of the Food and Mood Centre at Deakin University, Australia. Those selected to participate in the study had been experiencing symptoms of depression but did not have any comorbid physical or mental conditions that would complicate evaluating their moods or that would prevent them from modifying their diet.

Through random selection, the participants were split into two groups. Participants in one group met regularly, one-on-one, with a member of the study team to discuss subjects that they enjoyed but that were not related to their depression and that were not emotional. Known as "befriending," this social support process is offered in some countries (including the United Kingdom) to those suffering from a mental illness. Unsurprisingly perhaps, the mentally ill tend to have smaller social support networks, and the networks that they have tend, to a large extent, to be made up of mental health professionals and other mentally ill individuals. Befriending connects mentally ill individuals with nonprofessional volunteers to cultivate companionship and, as such, to provide ongoing support.[2]

The second group in the SMILEs study met with an accredited practicing dietitian to receive nutritional guidance. These participants were encouraged to follow a Modified Mediterranean Diet, which included vegetables, legumes, fresh fruits, nuts, whole grains, extra virgin olive oil, and fish. At the end of the study, only 8 percent of those in the befriending group met the criteria for remission of mental illness while 30 percent of participants in the dietary group met the criteria.[3]

Takeaway

Learn to cook. Instead of routinely eating out, ordering in, or consuming prepackaged foods, which might contain all kinds of fillers and ingredients that are not optimal for health, make your own meals with fresh, natural ingredients. Not only will this be cheaper in most cases, cooking your own food will give you greater control over the quality of food that you consume.

Cook foods from your childhood and you might find long-forgotten memories coming back to you that can be valuable to your personal growth, reminding you that things may have been a little different from what you remember. Cook new foods, perhaps from other cultures, and you will learn something new. Cook your own food and you will enjoy the feeling of having put thought and effort into making it yourself rather than having unthinkingly picked up and consumed some prepackaged food that is often quickly followed by feelings of guilt and self-critical thoughts of having given in to cravings or laziness.

PHYSICAL TRAINING

Regular physical exercise is essential for bodily health and mental well-being. Besides helping us to stay in shape—or even to improve the aesthetics of our body—exercise boosts energy, improves the quality of sleep, can improve sexual activity, and can help combat certain diseases.[4]

Moreover, exercise also heightens levels of dopamine and serotonin, causing individuals to feel good mentally after working out, and helping to fend off stress and feelings of low energy and enthusiasm. The post-workout "high" is linked to the endocannabinoid system.[5] The prefrontal cortex and amygdala have a significant number of receptors for endocannabinoids, a type of neurotransmitter (molecule) similar to cannabinoids in cannabis.[6]

Notably, many CEOs work out on a daily basis, often early in the morning, partly for the physical and mental benefits and partly to have some quiet time away from demanding and quickly changing professional environments.

However, losing excess fat and gaining muscle are probably the main reasons why people start exercising. Before we look at being overweight, though, we must note that, while less common in the West, being underweight has its own health risks due to the body not receiving the necessary nutrients. Health and wellness problems associated with being underweight include a constant feeling of tiredness, hair loss, osteoporosis, anemia, and, in women, irregular menstruation and giving birth prematurely. However, while around 2 percent of Americans over the age of twenty are underweight,[7] over 40 percent of the U.S. population is now obese.[8] And that number is rising.

We often think of fat merely as a fuel that the body will burn off through exercise or daily activity, but the fat cell is an endocrine organ, and it secretes hormones that affect the health of the individual. And notably, visceral fat produces a higher proportion of molecules that can create health problems such as cardiovascular disease and insulin resistance,[9] a precursor to type 2 diabetes.[10]

Hormones are essential to health. But men and women differ significantly in regard to estrogen and testosterone. Estrogen (sometimes called "the female hormone") is far higher in women than in men. Testosterone (sometimes called "the male hormone") is far higher in young men than in women. At puberty, testosterone is responsible for deepening the voice, causes hair to grow on the chest, and builds muscle. Later, it helps maintain muscle and bone mass and sexual drive.[11]

At nineteen, the average, healthy male will have somewhere between 240 and 950 nanograms per deciliter of blood, while the testosterone level of a healthy female of the same age will be many times lower, remaining only in the double digits.[12] While women experience a sudden decline in estrogen and progesterone during menopause, testosterone levels in men decline steadily over the decades, usually beginning after thirty or the early forties.[13]

At a certain point in the decline—dubbed the "male menopause" or the "andropause"—men can experience a loss of physical strength, muscle shrinkage, an absence of sexual desire, a lack of drive and ambition, and even depressive moods.[14] However, among those men who are able to stay physically and mentally fit, testosterone levels remain high—even into old age.[15] And, significantly, even where the testosterone levels have declined, physical exercise and proper diet will help to reverse this, boosting testosterone in men.

Takeaway

Think about your level of fitness now. How long does it take you to walk a mile? Are you out of breath or does your heart race when you walk? Do you see a lot of subcutaneous fat on your body or are you relatively slim? How many push-ups can you do before you need to rest?[16]

It is important that you assess your capabilities realistically instead of pretending that you can do more than you can.

Think about your fitness goals as well. What is your aim? To maintain your health? To be a bit more physically flexible? To lose fat? Or to gain muscle? Your answer might mean the difference between walking and yoga, light exercise, or weight lifting.

It can be difficult to create an appropriate physical training schedule, perform all of the exercises correctly so you avoid injuries, and stay motivated over the months and years. Find a professional physical trainer with whom you can begin a regular routine of physical training. Don't avoid gentle exercises such as walking, which can be highly beneficial for your health.

SLEEP

Getting little sleep is sometimes seen as a marker of commitment among corporate employees and entrepreneurs who may feel that they need to be working all the time. However, lack of sleep can lead to impulsivity and unnecessary risk-taking.[17] It can also negatively affect memory and lead to poor judgment more generally.[18] Moreover, because REM sleep is important for creativity, a lack of sleep can impair our ability to be creative, which includes problem-solving.[19] And of course, decision-making and creativity are essential to business and to navigating our increasingly complicated world in general.

Adequate nightly sleep of between seven to nine hours for adults[20] is essential for physical health and strength as well as mental well-being. In regard to the physical body, when we sleep, our pituitary gland (located at the base of the brain) produces human growth hormone. This hormone is responsible for growth in almost every organ and tissue in the body, helping children to grow taller and to develop stronger bones and cartilage and helping adults "to maintain normal body structure" throughout the rest of life.[21]

Lack of sleep has been associated with major health risks, including type 2 diabetes, obesity, Alzheimer's disease, and cardiovascular disease, as well as depression.[22] Making losing weight and getting—or staying—healthy more difficult, snacking and food cravings also increase when we do not get adequate sleep.[23] And food cravings tend to drive us toward unhealthy and especially sweet and sugary snacks.

Sleep plays a significant role in learning. A study by two MIT professors involving one hundred students found that both a lack of sleep and irregular sleep correlated with lower grades. Going to bed at a regular time and getting enough sleep during the period of learning is what made the difference. Hence, students with irregular sleep patterns, but who got a comparable amount of sleep to higher scoring students (sometimes going to bed earlier, sometimes later), still scored lower.[24] And trying to compensate for poor sleeping habits by getting a good night's sleep before an important event such as a test had no effect.

As such, although feeling rested and awake is undeniably an advantage over feeling exhausted and sleepy on a particular day, more important is the role of sleep in the learning process and, most especially, in memorization, information recall, critical thinking, and problem-solving. In one study, students were woken up during the night and asked to solve anagram puzzles. Notably, those woken during REM sleep (rapid eye movement sleep; the stage of sleep in which we tend to dream) solved 15 to 35 percent more puzzles than those woken up during non-REM sleep (the first stage of sleep, shallower than the REM stage).[25] Instead of forcing yourself to get little sleep, thinking it is some kind of badge of a dedicated employee or entrepreneur, consider getting enough sleep as integral to cultivating the right mindset for decision-making, creativity, and leadership.

Considering the importance of sleep to creativity, it is perhaps unsurprising that the master of surrealist painting Salvador Dali deliberately cultivated his sleep patterns before setting to work on a new painting. Dali would begin by sleeping deeply,[26] not only to help him cultivate a state of physical and mental "calm" when awake but to solve the painting's "subtle and complicated technical problems" during his hours of sleep.[27] We'll look at Dali's process very soon.

Takeaway

Make sure to regularly get enough sleep. If you can't get adequate sleep, acknowledge it; don't take on more than you can handle, and, if possible, leave decision-making until you're properly rested.

DEEP CONVERSATION

Close friendships are less common today than they were even a few decades ago.[28] Consequently, we have fewer people in our lives with whom we can discuss important matters.[29] Yet, meaningful conversations are essential to our well-being.

Psychologist Matthias Mehl at the University of Arizona wanted to explore how small talk (the exchange of trivial information) and more substantive conversations (about things that really mattered to those conversing) affect our happiness. He studied 79 undergraduate students (49 female, 30 male), audio recording 30-second snippets of their lives every 12.5 minutes over four days. The results showed that the happiest participants in the study spent less time alone and more time conversing with other people. And they spent substantially less time engaging in small talk and had "twice as many substantive conversations" as the least happy participants in the study.[30]

The brain changes when we converse in a meaningful way. During a conversation between two people, the brainwaves synchronize, creating "a connection between the two brains."[31] Moreover, positive, meaningful conversations boost the production of neurotransmitters and hormones such as dopamine, oxytocin, and endorphins, changing the body's chemistry.[32]

Notably, conversation, dialogue, or dialectic is an essential part of the relationship between tutor and student in traditional higher education, between priest and layman in religion, and guru and disciple in some spiritual traditions, as well as in therapy, hypnotherapy, consulting hypnotism, and mentoring. And of course, it is essential to nurture close friendships, especially, perhaps, during difficult times.

However, do not mistake complaining for substantial conversation, and do not allow yourself to fixate on the negative, blaming other people or groups of people for your situation, casting yourself as a victim. People often flock together to indulge their weaknesses. Instead, get into the habit of focusing on the positive and on the possible, even as you acknowledge life's challenges. Making a habit of concentrating on the positive and on what possible actions you can take to improve your circumstances helps to reduce stress.[33] Notably, Mastermind group sessions, intended to help members better themselves in some way, often open with a statement of principles, followed by each member of the group relating a piece of "good news."[34]

Takeaway

Cultivate relationships that enable you to discuss ideas, especially in relation to self-development, personal and professional. On those occasions when you need to discuss challenges or difficulties you are facing, empower yourself by steering the subject to potential solutions so you can contemplate the best way forward together.

DEEP READING

Entrepreneurs and CEOs read more books. While roughly one-quarter of American adults have not read a book in the last year, and while the average American reads twelve books a year,[35] Bill Gates reads fifty a year.[36] And like Elon Musk, he believes that reading is part of his success.[37]

Reading should open our minds to new ideas, possibilities, and potential. It should both stir our imagination and help us to think rationally. It should help us to understand ourselves. And it should help us to understand other people—including those who are different from us.

Unfortunately, the education system today often teaches people what to think rather than how to think. Media and social media encourage us to skim or speed read articles and to merely unquestioningly consume the latest opinion. And we, in turn, often read today's op-ed piece or this hour's news article not to really learn or gather new information but to reinforce our opinions.

Our modern and rather shallow way of reading sharply contrasts with the classical approach, which required the individual to reflect on what was written and think about it to understand what was being said, why it was being said, what it implied, and whether it was true or not.

Of course, in the premodern era, the average individual did not have a choice of hundreds, thousands, or millions of books to read. At most, one had a sacred book (the Bible, the Torah, or the Qur'an, etc.). This is still the case in some parts of the world. Yet the individual often knew that book by heart and could recite it chapter and verse. They thought about it deeply and saw how it revealed human condition and the vicissitudes of life and gave hope.

In Christian monasticism, there is a practice called *lectio divina* (literally "divine reading"). Guigo, a twelfth-century Carthusian monk, described the stages of lectio divina.[38] In the first stage (*lectio*, "reading"), an individual would read a passage of the Bible slowly, reflecting on it as they read. In the second stage (*meditatio*, "reflection"), they would contemplate the meaning of the passage that was just read. In the third stage (*oratio*, "speech"), the disciple would leave thinking and reflecting aside, letting the heart "speak" to God, while remaining silent. In the fourth and last stage (*contemplatio*, "contemplation"), the disciple would listen to their inner voice, intuition, or conscience—or what they believed to be the voice of God. And they would allow themself to be transformed by it.

It is one thing to gloss over words on a page without thinking about what they mean and forgetting them almost immediately. It is another to contemplate them deeply and to find profound meaning in a few lines of writing precisely because you have contemplated them deeply.

Takeaway

You don't need to follow the stages of lectio divina. Simply read a passage of a book, contemplate it, read it again, allow your mind to be quiet, and read and contemplate it again. Allow yourself to imagine and daydream about the meaning of the text, as well. Think about parallels and unexpected connections to your other areas of interest. Reading a passage in this way will prove more valuable to you than speed reading or skimming an entire book. Lastly, read subjects outside your specialist field of study or particular interests. Connections and insights can often be found in seemingly unlikely places.

RITUAL

In his book *Two Birds in a Tree*, economist and CEO of strategic consulting firm InnovaStrat Ram Nidumolu describes performing the traditional Hindu ritual after his father's passing. As the eldest son, the duty had fallen to Ram, who had flown from the United States to his home country of India. Over a period of twelve days, Ram had to perform different rituals according to an age-old formula. During that period, he found that, in his own words, "the rituals deepened key aspects of my individual identity profoundly by promoting a sense of belonging that transcended time and space."[39]

The ancient process, says Ram, "prepared you to think of individuals before and after you, as well as levels of hierarchy within your larger context (such as family, community, society, humanity, nature, and ultimately Being)." In other words, through performing these rituals, the economist and CEO found himself conscious of being interconnected with both the past and the future, as well as with the living ecosystem of family, community, nature, and so on.[40] It is counterintuitive to devote part of a book on business to ancient rituals, but through them, Ram saw clear lessons for business leaders today. He tells us,

> My experience with death rituals showed me how personal value came from a sense of identity with an ancestral lineage, as well as a shared purpose that gave deep satisfaction when the rituals were accomplished. This was intentional. Rituals such as those conducted around birth, marriage, death, and a host of other events, bound human beings to one another and to Being in ancient societies. Their core purpose was to provide meaning to ordinary human life, one that was deep, consistent, and engaged with the world.
>
> Being-centered leadership can similarly provide this identity and meaning to business work for its practitioners. This is because it can lead to a sense of vital engagement and alignment with different levels of the larger context (for example, team, company, society, humanity, nature, and ultimately Being) of a business leader.[41]

By "Being-centered leadership" Ram means leadership that recognizes the interconnectedness between individuals, communities, and nature, which—although sometimes invisible—is mutually sustaining. It requires thinking and acting holistically.[42]

It is often claimed that drinking a cup of coffee in the morning is a "ritual," but this represents a modern confusion about the nature of ritual. Perhaps drinking coffee in the morning is just a habit or a slight addiction. Certainly, few coffee drinkers see anything transcendent in the act. Our word *ritual* derives from the Latin *ritus*, meaning a "religious ceremony or observance." A ritual turns us away from our petty, everyday concerns and toward something greater: the sacred, the soul, the cosmos, our ancestors, and so on.

However, ritual, with its prescribed actions, does not necessarily equate to conformity of thought. In ancient Greece, citizens were free to view the gods and goddesses in different and even contrary ways. Hence, some ancient Greeks viewed them as mere metaphors while others believed in them in the most literal way. Regardless of their beliefs about their deities, all Greek citizens participated in the same rituals to them, and they did so with the same seriousness of attitude. Unsurprisingly then, it has been theorized that rituals "promote group survival."[43] And notably, many religious groups have survived for thousands of years.

Seasonal or annual rituals are also important to religious communities. Today the idea of waiting for a certain time of year to celebrate seems unnecessarily stoic. As noted before, we are able to indulge our senses and our cravings twenty-four hours a day. Yet such a lifestyle leaves the individual deeply unsatisfied. As we have said, the only thing we cannot have today is anticipation.

In pre-Christian Rome, the populace reveled during the celebration of Saturnalia. It was a time of feasting, socializing, gift-giving, gambling, and louche behavior. But it was celebrated for only one week out of the year, during December. Such behavior would not have been tolerated during the rest of the year. During the medieval period, Christmas was celebrated for twelve days. In our time, it is usually celebrated for only one or two days, though with eating special food, gift-giving, carol singing, and decorating the home with lights and a Christmas tree—the latter, at least, being a survival of an ancient pagan tradition.

During the Islamic celebration of Eid Al-Fitr, which usually lasts three days, families come together, the home is traditionally decorated with lanterns, and sweet pastries are served. There are, of course, many other comparable annual rituals, some of which go back to pre-Christian or to pre-Islamic times, such as Harvest Festival in England and the new year festival of Nowruz in Iran. Typically, we find that cultures have several festivals throughout the year. Instead of living for the weekend, get in touch with your own traditional, seasonal celebrations; look forward to them, and do something—such as eating a special meal or celebrating with friends—to mark them. Or create an event for close friends once a month to celebrate—and just as important, to look forward to it.

The premodern person had no opportunity to indulge their every whim on their own, all day, every day. But unlike many modern individuals, they had something to look forward to with family and community. They could recall experiencing them as a child with their mother and father and could, in turn, experience them with their own children. Through such rituals, the individual gained an appreciation of time and of being a link in a chain between ancestors and descendants.

Even on a more mundane level, of course, looking forward to a positive event elevates our mood and helps us cope with stress.[44] Such annual rituals as we have mentioned were prepared for weeks or longer in advance, requiring participants to delay gratification. For example, in England, the Christmas pudding was traditionally made a whole year before the celebration. Unsurprisingly perhaps, while continually indulging our cravings reduces dopamine, thus requiring more and more stimulation for us to feel the same effect, delaying gratification increases dopaminergic neurons in the midbrain,[45] the main source of dopamine in our central nervous system.[46]

Ritual reconnects us to the past and future and to those we love and respect. And it reminds us of the connection between the sacred and the mundane. To the premodern peoples the earthly was reflected in the heavenly realm and vice versa. A god could wander through a town in disguise. The planets were believed to affect the personality, health, and even the destinies of ordinary people. The relic of a saint could heal the sick. All of this seems ridiculous to the modern individual, but rituals require us to set aside time to reflect on the ideal.* And rituals, as Ram Nidumolu recognized, are about our duties.

Those duties may be to our family or community. They may be to ourselves—to stop indulging our excuses and do what we need to do to improve ourselves and our behavior. And those duties may even be to a god. In Hinduism, as in some other faiths, an offering might be made before a statue of a deity each month or even every day.

---

*From the Latin *idealis*, "existing in idea," the Latin *idea* refers to the Platonic idea or archetype.

Takeaway

Whether you are religious or not, schedule time to pay homage to the ideal through ordinary activities. Here are just four suggestions:

1. If you are working toward losing weight, getting toned, or putting on muscle, dedicate your physical training sessions, yoga sessions, Pilates, or weight training to the ideal form (perhaps that of a Greek god whose image you have seen in sculptures). Contemplate the beauty of this ideal body, which you have yet to attain. And consider the discipline required to be an act of sacrifice to your higher ideal.
2. Even when times are busy, make time to meet valued friends. And when you meet, recognize that it is a sacred moment that demands your full attention. Be generous, listen intently, and speak earnestly, talk of meaningful things, and speak with encouragement. To be fully present, as you are on your way to meet your friend, think to yourself, *This moment will never come again.*
3. Make the traditional food your parents made you when you were growing up. Appreciate the time and love that they put into it. And recognize the connection that has been established through the generations, from ancestors to great-grandparents, grandparents to parents, from your parents to you, and perhaps from you to your children. Eat slowly and take your time to really taste the food.
4. Sip water throughout the day, and each time you take a sip, focus all your attention on the sensation of the water in your mouth and trickling down your throat. Say to yourself, *I drink this water in honor of my true self that I am working toward becoming.* Then recall your greatest aims in life: to get healthier, to work on your art or business, or to be more outgoing and social, and so on. Whatever it is, think about it for a few seconds. See yourself performing the necessary tasks, enjoying it,

and achieving your aims. This is especially valuable if you have aims in your life but are busy and can understandably be swept up by daily tasks.

CONTEMPLATION

Since the Age of Enlightenment, the West especially has come to fetishize the intellect and rational thinking. As we have seen already, prior to the modern era thinking was divided into ratio (rational thought) and intellectus (higher knowledge through contemplation). Ratio, the lower type of thinking, was the workhorse of the mind. Specific problems could be tackled and perhaps solved through the active application of rational thinking. But it was through intellectus that the individual perceived existence holistically. In contrast to ratio, intellectus is receptive and is related to contemplation and intuition.

It is essential for us to take the time to contemplate not only our thoughts and beliefs but also beauty. The twentieth-century mystic G. I. Gurdjieff regarded the impressions that we take in as a kind of food. What we see around us shapes our psyche and can make us feel energized and enthusiastic or depressed and defeated. Note that prisons always confine the prisoner in a very plain and often very ugly environment with limited or no personal images allowed to be displayed, with the prisoner having limited or no ability to see nature or even the sky.

Takeaway

There are three main ways in which we can see beauty—in nature (including animals), culture, and in other people. Even if you live in the city, get out into nature periodically if possible. Walk or hike and allow the mind to quiet as you focus on the natural environment. If you can't spend time outside of an urban environment, visit a local park frequently and appreciate the relative quiet, open space, sky, trees, and whatever nature can be found there. Try to spend at least thirty minutes outside each day.

In regard to culture, if you live in a city, visit or go for walks through its most beautiful areas and appreciate the architecture and the surroundings. If you can, travel widely so that you get different perspectives on life, experience different cultures, and develop a deeper understanding of history and the evolution of cultures. Appreciate the time and care that went into creating everything from sculptures to everyday objects such as plates or bowls, which were often highly decorative. Visit art galleries and look at art. Think about your own living space aesthetically.

Lastly, in regard to people, notice the aesthetics in people's comportment (how they stand, talk, and interact with other people) and become conscious of what is attractive and what is repellent, what exudes inner strength, confidence, and attentiveness, and what exposes weakness, arrogance, and a fragile ego. While boasting, vulgar talk, and constantly chasing sex are often presented as confident behaviors they are not only ugly but signal inner weakness. The individual masks insecurities by boasting and displays of arrogance. The vulgar-talking individual is probably too stupid to think deeply, to reflect, or to speak thoughtfully. And the individual who is always chasing sex is probably addicted to it and perhaps fearful of relationships. Lacking self-control, those who are always chasing sex will betray even a long-term friendship for momentary pleasure and an ego boost.

In contrast, a successful and confident individual takes their time to give advice to someone younger and less confident. A strong individual helps those who are weaker. An intelligent and knowledgeable person listens attentively to others, even if they are less intelligent and educated. Such behavior reveals a certain inner strength and good character. The combination of strength and kindness or thoughtfulness is highly attractive.

SELF-HYPNOSIS

The origins of hypnotism are often traced back more than two millennia to the sleep temples of ancient Egypt under Imhotep (ca. twenty-seventh century BCE), and the asclepieion of ancient Greece. Functioning as hospitals, patients would be placed in a trancelike condition in the Egyptian sleep temples. Then their dreams would be analyzed and appropriate treatments would be administered. It is possible that many ailments healed thereby were of a psychological nature.[47] Similarly, dedicated to the god of medicine, Asclepius, the asclepieion healed patients through incubation—sleeping and experiencing visions or dreaming.[48]

But hypnotism has also influenced much in the modern world from psychoanalysis to neuro-linguistic programming (the latter being partly based on the work of hypnotherapist Milton Erickson), from the positive thinking movement to the training of professional athletes, and from spirituality to the sales profession.

Psychoanalysts Sigmund Freud (1856–1939) and Carl Jung (1875–1961) both practiced hypnotism early in their careers. The founder of the New Thought or positive thinking movement, Phineas Quimby (1802–1866), was a practicing hypnotist, as was one of the movement's more influential thinkers, Émile Coué (1857–1926). More recently, hypnotism has been used in the training of professional athletes, including world champion golfer Tiger Woods,[49] as well as world champion boxers Mike Tyson, Frank Bruno,[50] and Ken Norton.[51]

Hypnosis and meditation can feel very alike. However, there are some very significant differences. Most importantly, hypnosis is integrated into daily life. Richard Bandler has said that "at some level or another, everything is hypnosis." He believes that people are always moving through different trances. "They have their work trances," he says, "their relationship trances, their driving trances, their parenting trances, and a whole collection of problem trances."[52]

In meditation, the meditator tries to ignore or to block out thoughts, usually by focusing on the breath, and usually it only takes a few second for thoughts to intrude again. In contrast, hypnotism refines and focuses thinking. It cultivates the appropriate mindset. And it takes this approach for a good reason. The average individual thinks between 12,000 and 50,000 thoughts each day.[53]

The vast majority of these thoughts are, of course, mundane and repetitive. We thought them (or something very much like them) the day before, and the day before that. These are thoughts about how to get from A to B, what to eat for lunch, what movie we might like to watch tonight, and so on. Yet with our brain constantly active, in details both large and small, we are continually reinforcing our self-identity, including our sense of what we are, or are not, capable of achieving, and what we do, or do not, deserve.

Often, we are not really conscious of the character of our thoughts and do not notice how, with a negative mindset, we defeat ourselves in life. Instead of facing our weaknesses, fears, and laziness we often excuse them. Worse, many individuals find meaning and a sense of self-righteousness in their own character weaknesses, blaming circumstances, parents, or people they have never met—as if they are far more important than they really are.

Beginning Self-Hypnosis

As we begin to fall asleep at night, we pass through a stage called hypnagogia and as we begin to wake up in the morning we enter the state of hypnopompia. It is in these states that we often experience dreaming. From the ancient Greek god Hypnos, the *hypno* part of these terms means, literally, "sleep." As their names suggest, these states are similar to that of hypnosis. Hypnopompia, hypnagogia, and hypnosis are usually characterized by deep relaxation combined with an awareness of our thoughts and openness to suggestion.

There are really four reasons that we might want to practice self-hypnosis: (1) relaxation, (2) inspiration, (3) visualization of future scenarios or possible scenarios, and (4) dreaming. Although not really the focus of this book, dreaming can occur during self-hypnosis after becoming so relaxed that you enter a state of hypnagogia and fall asleep, usually for only a few seconds at a time. Let's look at the other three reasons:

Relaxation

By relaxation we are not talking about time outside of work, watching a movie or passively consuming some other form of entertainment. We are talking about deeply relaxing both the body and the mind.

Constant stress or constantly being on the go, relaxing only superficially, can contribute to serious health problems. However, routinely practicing entering a state of deep relaxation can have significant benefits including better sleep, lower blood pressure, and even an improved immune system.[54]

A 2009 study by Harvard University found that more "disease-fighting genes" were active in long-term, routine "practitioners of relaxation methods" than in individuals who did not practice any type of relaxation techniques. These genes helped to protect practitioners against a range of maladies including high blood pressure, rheumatoid arthritis, and even infertility. Moreover, the study also found that disease-fighting genes began to turn on after consistently practicing relaxation techniques for only two months.[55] A more recent study by Harvard-affiliated Massachusetts General Hospital found that after a year, the consistent practice of "relaxation-response techniques" such as mindfulness exercises, meditation, yoga, and prayer reduced the need for healthcare services by 43 percent.[56]

Most people enjoy being in a state of hypnosis because it is usually very relaxing. If you don't want to practice self-hypnosis for any other reason, make it or some other deep relaxation method a part of a health and wellness routine.

Inspiration

In 1831, Mary W. Shelley recalled that her most famous novel, *Frankenstein*, began with her laying down one night:

> When I placed my head upon my pillow, I did not sleep, nor could I be said to think. My imagination, unbidden, possessed and guided

me, gifting the successive images that arose in my mind with a vividness far beyond the usual bounds of reverie.[57]

As soon as Shelley began to relax, she was flooded with images and inspiration for her literary work. Again, during periods of cultivating his sleep patterns, Dali would practice what he called "slumber with a key." The artist would recline in a chair while holding a heavy key between his thumb and index finger over an upturned plate placed on the floor. At some point, he would of course fall asleep and the key would fall onto the plate, waking him with the sound of metal hitting the china. Dali's intention here was to experience a very brief period of sleep.[58]

We have probably all experienced our mind racing as we lay down to sleep, of course. Sometimes this can be caused by an individual wrestling with fear or wallowing in anger. However, finding ourselves suddenly inspired and flooded with novel ideas is not unusual.

As you practice self-hypnosis, and enter a state of deep calm and relaxation, you might find answers to creative problems suddenly coming to you. Or you might find yourself struck by inspiration in some other way. If you try to remember the inspiration or solutions until after your session, you might well forget it. Keep a journal and pen by you. If a creative solution to a problem or some other inspiration occurs to you, stop and write it down. The muses often strike before you have entered a deep state of hypnosis and not long after you have relaxed your mind and body.

Indeed, you have undoubtedly experienced something like this many times, at least on a more mundane level. You can probably remember trying to recall the name of someone or something during a conversation and trying to force yourself to remember, perhaps mentally going through the alphabet as a prompt for the word you were seeking. Then, as you gave up and thus relaxed, the name of the person or object hit you, almost like a force from somewhere else. The intellect has its limits. Once we relax, what we cannot discover consciously will often appear out of our subconscious.

Visualization

Many people practice visualization, of course, but they generally focus their eyes even as the eyelids are closed, often pointing their gaze upward and inward, toward the eyebrows. This is likely to keep the individual from entering a state of either hypnosis or hypnagogia.

We have mentioned Dali. In the final stage of his sleep cultivation process, he would take the eyes of a cooked sea perch and place them on a book in front of him before he was about to fall asleep. Then he would focus his attention on them, relaxing his gaze so that the two eyes on the book appeared to merge and become one. Eventually Dali would fall asleep, but we relax our gaze when we daydream or enter hypnosis.[59] Notably, hypnotists have sometimes used similar methods as Dali, such as swinging a pendulum in front of the eyes, which soon becomes too tiring to keep watching.

Today, of course, most people are sharply focused on a computer screen and on a smartphone for virtually every minute of their waking life, constantly consuming information. Especially if you are a creative individual (including an entrepreneur or a CEO who needs to problem solve), leave your phone aside for a period of time each day, relax your gaze, and allow yourself to think and even to daydream. If you are routinely taking in information, you must allow yourself the space to contemplate that information and to enable novel ideas and solutions to emerge from your own consciousness.

Takeaway

To make beginning self-hypnosis as simple as possible, make use of the hypnopompic state. As you begin to awaken each morning, even before your eyes are open, your brain is already switching into a well-worn, if unconscious, pattern of behavior. Notice that even before you are fully awake you are not as relaxed as you might assume. Even before your eyes open in the morning, it is likely that you will already be tensing parts of your face. This is habitual and involuntary. The first thing you can do in the morning, then, is notice this tension and—still half asleep—allow your face and body to relax.

In the New Thought or positive thinking movement, these times of day and their states of consciousness are often used for saying affirmations or for visualizing the future that the individual is hoping for and is working toward. Such visualizations are usually of the individual in the future and how they look (e.g., dress and posture) and feel (e.g., confident or happy) achieving, or having achieved, a specific aim. As you begin to make use of the hypnopompic and hypnagogic states, focus on one aim at a time. Focus on it every day over several days or weeks at a time. Focus on an aim that is desirable, possible for you to achieve, and that—with positive self-talk and self-discipline—you will routinely dedicate your time and energy to.

However, do not let your self-hypnosis be something that is added on to your day for a few minutes and then forgotten about. Cultivate calm throughout your day. Even as you acknowledge problems in your life, focus on the positive during the day. Give your attention to solutions and work toward them. See the good in other people and respect their good qualities so that you might eventually embody them yourself. Even if you only do one small thing each day, work toward improving yourself and your life every day.

5

The Language of Enchantment

IN 1991, GERALD RATNER was the chairman and chief executive of Ratners Jewellery, then the world's largest jewelry retailer and a household name in Great Britain. Owning both a helicopter and private jet, Ratner himself was flying high—literally and figuratively. He also had a chauffeur-driven Bentley, a house in Mayfair (one of London's most expensive neighborhoods), and another house in Berkshire for a countryside escape.

Ratner had engineered his company's meteoric rise by doing things differently from other jewelry retailers and, most especially, by making the vibe a lot friendlier to customers. Unusual for British jewelers, Ratner played pop music inside his shops and displayed fashionable earrings and chains in their windows rather than expensive diamond rings.

Everything was going to plan. But chaos has a way of intervening. Ratner was invited to give a talk at the Institute of Directors' annual convention at the Royal Albert Hall. Well-known for his wit, during his speech, he threw in a couple jokes, unwisely poking a bit of fun at a decanter and a pair of earrings that his shops were selling. The jokes got an "enormous laugh" from the audience. But, the next day, the tabloids reported the jokes. Britain was in economic recession at the time and now with the jokes considered in a very different context, the public was furious. People boycotted Ratner's shops. Over one hundred had to be closed. Employees were made unemployed, no doubt plunging many into chaos. And the share price of Ratners Jewelry plummeted to almost nothing (technically, to two pence—roughly four U.S. cents at the time). Two years later, what was left of the company was quietly renamed "the Signet Group."[1]

What we say matters. What we say can have a profound effect on our lives, for good or ill. Perhaps unsurprisingly then, in antiquity language was intimately tied to magic. Thoth was the ancient Egyptian god of both magic and writing. Even in the most ordinary environment, however, a master of language can seduce individuals and even entire crowds with their words. That surely is magic.

Sometimes the magic is in the passion and conviction with which the words are spoken. Sometimes it is the authority of the speaker. Sometimes it is in the tone and meter. And sometimes it is in the word choice—the sound of the words and whether or not they are the kind of words we would use. Would you rather be taken to a restaurant that is beautiful or one that is pulchritudinous? Like the rest of us, you'd probably prefer the beautiful even though the little-used *pulchritudinous* is just a synonym for beautiful, albeit the ugliest-sounding synonym in the English language. The philosopher Ernst Cassirer (1874–1945) says the following:

> If we study the development of human speech, we find that in the history of civilization the word fulfills two entirely different functions. To put it briefly we may term these functions the semantic and the magical use of the word. Even among the so-called primitive languages the semantic function of the word is never missing; without it there could be no human speech. But in primitive societies the magic word has a predominant and overwhelming influence. It does not describe things or relations of things; it tries to produce effects and to change the course of nature.[2]

However, says Cassirer, "Curiously enough, all this recurs in our modern world." He notes that in his own time, when reading a book on economic, historical, or philosophical problems, "New words have been coined; and even the old ones are used in a new sense; they have undergone a deep change of meaning."[3] The redefining of old words, it seems to be implied, was intended not only to purge the established meaning but to prevent questioning and thinking about the new agenda—whatever it may be.

While we can find parallels in antiquity, it is essential for us to understand how language is used in our own age and especially how it is used to enchant, persuade, convince, empower, disempower, and change minds. We must understand, too, how our own internal dialogues or self-talk affects our consciousness, shapes our worldview, and causes us to make particular choices, and to repeat the same mistakes, over and over again. We live in a world that is increasingly a competition between the mass and the individual, between dumbing down and stepping up, and between the techniques of propaganda and our own sense of who we are.

One of the most obvious attempts to use words in a magical way can be found in certain segments of academia and, perhaps more especially, in those college-educated individuals who emulate intellectuals in order to imply that their thoughts have plunged depths entirely unknown to the average person. Here everyday words are repeated unnecessarily frequently, drawing attention to them while at the same time creating a sense of strangeness and unfamiliarity, as if the word is a kind of mantra or incantation. Often the suffix *-ness* is added to words, turning nouns and verbs into adjectives with the effect that we feel that we are discussing previously undetected invisible forces. Hence, instead of speaking of the quality of a place or of places, for example, an individual might speak of "placeness," "placelessness," and even "non-places," "locatedness," "situatedness," "at-homeness," and even "insideness." Analytical, yet isolated within the confines of academia, such language seems designed to hold the chaos of the world at bay.

Of course, just as car mechanics have their special terms, so do academics. But everyday terms, often with the definite article dropped or *ness* added at the end, are, as mentioned, used or misused by nonacademics to show how clever they are and to prevent questioning from any potential skeptics. This tactic and using more elevated and obscure terms in general is especially useful when the positions of the speaker are unpopular, provably wrong, lack evidence, or have simply not been thought through. Those who truly understand a subject can express their thoughts about it clearly and in simple terms. But by creating a monologue too boring to follow intently, such magic words intimidate the less educated and leave a large percentage of the population believing that they are listening to someone who is very clever and, therefore, should not be openly questioned.

Magic terminology is used elsewhere. You and I might say that a corporation has "lost money." However, the corporation would tell us that it has experienced "negative growth," which sounds neutral. Similarly, when a corporation lays off staff it is "restructuring."

Government and smartly dressed spin doctors frequently use similarly banal terms, also intended to make our eyes glaze over and our mind wander away from the bad news. *Charlie Foxtrot* is a military euphemism for a situation that has turned into chaos. Instead of talking about deaths of civilians an army or government spokesperson will use the euphemism *collateral damage* since this is more likely to—wrongly— evoke an image of mere financial loss or damaged property than what it really indicates: a pile of dead bodies. Similarly, most people will object to government lockdowns but fewer people will object to sheltering in place because, while the former sounds permanent and involuntary, the latter sounds temporary and voluntary as well as sensible. Who would object to sheltering from a danger? And doesn't *sheltering* sound rather cozy? Certainly, this is much better even than the more literal but authoritarian-sounding phrase "don't leave your home."

When an individual wants to avoid answering a question that might make them vulnerable to criticism or that requires them to reveal their innermost feelings, they will often talk in collective terms, invoking *you*, meaning people in general, or *we*, instead of using *I*. Asked about a situation in which an interviewee's actions were allegedly unethical or worse, someone might say, for example, "when you're in that situation" before speaking in generalities, rather than "when I was in that situation" and addressing specific details of what the individual either did or did not do. Speaking in generalities enables the individual to avoid implicating themselves, unless they are continually pressed to be more specific.

Deceptive language might also be laden with terms such as *inclusion*, *ownership*, *responsibility*, and so on, that imply that the speaker is highly moral. We assume that such words have real importance to the speaker because they are meaningful to us. But they are used abstractly, unrelated to any specific actions of the speaker, which are not mentioned since the speaker probably acted in ways contrary to what their statement suggests. Abstraction makes a person sound thoughtful and intelligent. And using positive words that we all agree with makes them appear likable, trustworthy, and even charismatic. When agreeing with the speaker, it is easy for an audience not to notice that person is effectively hiding behind rhetoric and is able to avoid revealing what they did or did not do.

Especially in a high-profile setting such as a television interview, people will often employ contemporary political buzzwords—especially those that are regarded as signifying the correct moral positions, since these are generally sacrosanct. This makes it difficult to question the speaker's intentions, at least without appearing to be a morally dubious character—which is precisely why such terms are used, and used so vaguely, without any mention of concrete actions taken by the speaker. Depending on the audience, these magic words might be *patriotism*, *robust deterrence*, and *law and order*, or *diversity*, *community*, and *safety*. It is the effect of the words that matter, not the words themselves. In a business setting, someone might use these, or they might talk of *teamwork*, *commitment*, *integrity*, and so on.

Although we will look at exceptions in a moment, magic words often fall into two camps: those with a very definite meaning and those that are vague. Those with more definite meanings tend to be associated with celebrities and brands, especially those that are known by a single word: Rihanna, Beyoncé, Slash, Elvis, Apple (instead of "Apple Inc."), Hershey's (not the Hershey Company), Coke (not Coca Cola), and so on. We call the celebrities *icons*, a term adopted from religion, where it referred to paintings or sculptures of saints—people who were believed to have the power to heal or answer prayers—and we call these brands *iconic brands*.

In regard to the use of vague but powerful words, in 2008, Shepard Fairey was drafted by the campaign team for then–presidential hopeful Barack Obama to design a campaign poster. Fairey created a red, white, blue, and navy portrait of the presidential candidate with the word *progress* underneath. However, Obama's campaign team thought that there were "troublesome connotations" with the word and expressed their concern to Fairey. In response, he changed it to *hope*.[4] The word and the poster became iconic.

But were voters supposed to hope for higher taxes (on people wealthier than them) to pay for education, environmental projects, and so on, or were they supposed to hope for lower taxes to stimulate the economy? Or something else? *Progress*, with its "troublesome connotations," would have suggested to some voters the kind of changes that they wouldn't like. But no possibility is excluded from *hope*. Even though it signifies change, no matter what an individual hopes for, it includes or appears to include them.

This was not the first time that *hope* had been used in a political campaign. Four years earlier, in the bid to be elected president and vice president, Democrats John Kerry and John Edwards had used the slogan "hope is on the way,"[5] which they turned into an almost hypnotic refrain at rallies, tagging it onto comments about various issues. Obama's single word slogan—"hope"—remains iconic. No one remembers the five-word slogan of Kerry and Edwards. Perhaps we have forgotten "hope is on the way" because this Democrat duo lost. But Kerry and Edwards also lost, in part, because their slogan failed to excite. There was just no real magic in it.

It is easy to understand when we see a face of a presidential candidate with the word *hope* underneath that the hope for the future is in the candidate winning. And, as we have said, the single word *hope* enables everyone to project their fantasies onto it. "Hope is on the way" just leaves us with a lot of questions: Where is the hope coming from? Does Kerry mean to suggest that he is the hope that he believes is on its way? Or is someone else the hope? If hope is on the way, isn't that already hope? And if it is, isn't hope already here? Or if hope isn't here, is the presidential hopeful actually hopeless?

Of course, usually one magic word isn't enough. We have to express ourselves through statements and arguments if we want to shape the way others think. But even a single change in word choice can make a difference because the words we choose not only inform the listener (e.g., about a particular event), they also interpret the subject being spoken about and subtly tell us what to think. Let's imagine that someone was at the scene of a crime. In some capacity or other, they spoke to the police about the crime and are now being questioned about this by a television interviewer. Let's think about three sentences with only one slight word change that the interviewer might say to the interviewee and what each statement implies:

1. "But you admitted that you were there."
2. "But you acknowledged that you were there."
3. "But you said that you were there."

Logically, the words *admitted, acknowledged*, and *said* all give us the exact same information: someone said something. But we are likely to interpret the guilt, innocence, and character of the individual very differently depending on which of these words is used.

In the first statement, *admitted* implies guilt. The individual has admitted being at the scene of the crime. In the view of the interviewer, he has gone some way to fully confessing but is still holding back. Now we just need him to admit to being the wrongdoer we have been looking for. From the first short sentence, then, we are likely to conclude that we are dealing with a criminal.

In the second statement, our hypothetical interviewer uses a more neutral term: *acknowledged*. Perhaps the police have been pressuring our imaginary interviewee and trying to blame them for the crime. The TV interviewer might be on the side of the interviewee, or at least wants to give this person a fair hearing. In contrast to the first example, by acknowledging being there, it is implied that the individual hasn't tried to hide anything. The interviewer believes that they have most likely been honest in their dealing with the police.

In the last statement, we might detect that the interviewer is a little frustrated with the investigating police. The individual has said that they were at the scene of the crime and they aren't being listened to. Possibly they are being wrongly blamed or perhaps their eyewitness testimony is being ignored by the police, who may be going after the wrong person.

But how many of us really pause to consider the word choice of news presenters, news articles, or op-eds and their nuances? Most people will either be swept up by the energy of the presenter or the language or will react against it because they don't like the media outlet. Do we really notice how ads are crafted to appeal to us instinctively rather than rationally? Usually we don't.

Such word choice as mentioned above may or may not be unconscious. In rhetoric—or to use a more modern term, persuasion—there are actual techniques for influencing the listener. One technique for this is *agnomination*, or rhyming two words in the same sentence. Common examples of this include "a friend in need is a friend indeed," "no pain, no gain," and "an apple a day keeps the doctor away." Agnomination has the power to make a statement repeatable, and when something is easy to repeat we are less inclined to question its validity. Notice that we almost always talk about the fight-or-flight response to a threat when the possible responses are the much less catchy fight, flight, freeze, or fawn.

When Hillary Clinton announced that she was running for president of the United States in 2007, she went for the big gun of agnomination: "I'm in, and I'm in to win."[6] Her declaration was carefully designed not only to present her as a winner from day one of her campaign but to be repeatable (she's in it to win it). However, successful political campaigns are about the voter, not the presidential hopeful. Clinton subsequently changed her slogan several times, going through such unmemorable war cries as "The strength and experience to make change happen," "Big challenges, real solutions: Time to pick a president," and "Turn up the heat; turn America around."[7] Turn up the heat on whom?

In contrast, Clinton's 2016 competitor, Donald Trump stuck with "make America great again"—a slogan that uses assonance or the repetition of a vowel sound (in this case, $\bar{a}$) to make it memorable. Notably, Trump's slogan and Clinton's "turn America around" both imply the same thing: we need to make America as powerful or prosperous as it was in the past. But while Trump's slogan focuses the listener on how great it will be, Clinton's has a sense both of going back and of hard work.

Because they can be culturally infectious, sales campaigns sometimes make use of this agnomination. Hence Energizer's slogan "No battery is stronger longer" and Boeing's "If it's not Boeing, I'm not going." Agnomination can be used to drive us toward a certain conclusion, either by presenting a choice in which only one option is really desirable or one is highly undesirable ("my way or the highway") or by articulating the conclusion. Chevrolet's post–World War II slogan "See the USA in your Chevrolet" implies that the car is so reliable we will be able to drive it across America without it breaking down and, as such, it is an extremely reliable car for just going from A to B every day.

During the closing remarks of the 1994–95 O. J. Simpson trial, defense lawyer Johnny Cochran famously instructed the jury that "If the glove doesn't fit, you must acquit." In this example of agnomination (using *fit* and *acquit*), Cochran boiled the case for the defense down to a single, memorable sentence. Not only would Cochran's comment have stuck in the jurors' minds, several jurors would have been bound to repeat it in deliberation. Just as importantly, jurors would also have imagined telling friends, family, and possibly even the press about the trial, which attracted massive amounts of media attention. Cochran's slogan not only gave them a lens through which the trial should be viewed but a talking point and an explanation for an innocent verdict. Of course, people are entirely capable of reasoning and ignoring catchy phrases, but such language is compelling.

During the fourth century BCE, Aristotle wrote *On Rhetoric: A Theory of Civic Discourse*, explaining the subject. For the ancient Greek philosopher, the power of rhetoric lay in *pathos, logos,* and *ethos* or emotional appeal, reasoned argument, and authority. If a person could appeal to the emotions of the listener, convince them of the veracity of their claims, and could demonstrate that their claims were made from a position of authority, then they would be convincing. In our current society, rational arguments come a distant second or third after feelings. This is especially the case in marketing, politics, and much that passes for education.

As already noted, to win people over emotionally, a speaker will often use *we*. "We must act" to protect our planet, our nation, or humanity from some terrible fate, it might be argued, even though the speaker often means that *you* must act, sometimes exempting themselves from making any personal sacrifice. If a vivid picture of an alleged impending disaster or a great victory can be painted through words, this will stir the emotions and will make people more likely to act. "Very persuasive individuals can orchestrate vivid images that influence both the preconception and mood of the listener," say Donald Moine and Kenneth Lloyd in *Unlimited Selling Power: How to Master Hypnotic Selling Skills*. "Highly skilled salespeople use 'word magic' to bring their prospects and customers to other worlds of sights and sounds and feelings."[8]

While voters might have believed in the authority (ethos) of a presidential candidate, some of the above-mentioned slogans don't present any real argument (logos) and worse—if the aim is to persuade—fail to connect emotionally (pathos) with the listener. This was undoubtedly the case with Kerry and Edwards's slogan. Instead, they relied on the hypnotic technique of repetition.

As Moine and Lloyd note, repetition and much else from hypnotism has entered into sales and marketing. While a hypnotist, in the process of helping their client to relax, might say softly and slowly, "Your eyelids are getting heavier, heavier, heavier," an ad for a brand might announce that "Our prices are low, low, low," they note.[9] However, such obvious repetition in marketing tends to be a technique used at the more bargain-basement end of the consumer spectrum. Premium and luxury brands prefer to create an image, even a mystique. This might be the case in politics as well. Chanting slogans tends to take place in street demonstrations, which most people find annoying at best.

Hypnotists pay close attention to their clients' use of language. When someone visits a hypnotist, it's usually because they haven't found a solution to a particular problem. And they usually haven't found the solution because the problem is not what they think it is. By paying attention to how an individual uses language, a hypnotist can often detect issues that they are being less than honest about—even with themself. Gently probing these areas can help someone to understand what is going on.

As we noted above, when an individual is probed about a sensitive subject, they will often try to evade answering directly and might generalize instead, speaking in terms of "you" and "we" instead of "I." People will also distort the facts or leave out certain information to make themselves look better. We'll look at this again shortly. An individual might exaggerate a problem. They might, for example, describe a particular situation as "impossible," "a disaster," or "a real pain" when in reality it is much less serious. In a sense, the individual is using magic words against themself.

If a person can instead come to see the situation under discussion as, for example, a mere challenge, or better still as their shot at personal success, which will inevitably lead them to a new enjoyment of life, they will find it easier to triumph over. We've spoken of chaos, but at this point, you should begin to think of change, disruption, upheaval, and the like as opportunity.

Chaos awaits the unprepared. Opportunity awaits the prepared. We have discussed the forces that govern societies and how to take advantage of them. And we have already explored techniques for personal and professional growth and persuasion. We will soon go deeper.

As you might imagine, hypnotists also look for positive words and descriptions, even if these are merely describing how the client would like to feel. Later, when the client is in hypnosis, the hypnotist might use these descriptions to get them to vividly see what they can achieve if they follow a particular course of action. We all have our own internal reference system. One client might say that she wants to feel "like a princess." Another might want to feel "like a rock star" or "like a million dollars."

We earlier spoke about emotionally powerful words being used dishonestly. It is essential to be aware of how people enchant us through language. Self-serving, manipulative individuals are often forced to move around, both professionally and in personal relationships, as people begin to notice incongruities between their speech and their actions and consequently begin to suspect their motives.

In general, success in life depends on relationships. Relationships require trust and trust requires honesty. However, honesty does not mean tactlessness or focusing on the negative. Rather than saying "your clothes are horrible and totally inappropriate," for example, we can suggest that someone would look "amazing" or would get more dates or more professional opportunities if they dressed a little differently, considering their other positive qualities. The most powerful language is both positive and truthful.

6
Self-Talk

DURING THE EARLY 1900s, while working in a pharmacy in Troyes, in the northwest of France, Émile Coué noticed that his patients recovered quicker if he praised the medicine that he was dispensing to them.[1] As is now widely recognized, our perception of a particular medicine can be a powerful factor in recovery. Coué, who had studied hypnotism under Ambroise-Auguste Liébeault only a few years earlier, understood this.[2]

Coué came to believe that "we constantly give ourselves unconscious autosuggestions,"[3] often negative and steeped in fear, which prevents us from living up to our potential and ultimately living the life that we would like to live. The antidote to this unconscious self-sabotage, Coué believed, is the *conscious* autosuggestion or what we might call "self-hypnosis." In a sense, like hypnotism, the conscious autosuggestion is an attempt to overwrite the old, unconscious programing.

Much of this programming will have been inculcated in childhood through parents, teachers, friends, and so on. But some of it will also be cultural or, we might say, propagandist. We have seen how techniques of rhetoric—or persuasion—are used in politics and marketing to make us feel favorably about a particular politician or product without pesky critical thinking having a chance to intervene.

While hypnotists see clients for a range of challenges, from confidence and performance to stress management, let's think about someone who wants to quit smoking or vaping. At some point, usually during the teenage years or early twenties, the individual had received the suggestion that they should smoke or vape. At first, smoking, especially, would have felt and tasted disgusting but the individual would have forced themself to persist because their friends smoked or because they had been influenced by advertisements for the product or by the presentation of smoking in the movies. Much the same applies to vaping and to other unwanted habits, of course.

As Coué recognized, however, a suggestion from an external source is not quite enough. To be effective the unconscious mind has to transform it into an autosuggestion.[4] Or to put it bluntly, the suggestion has to spark and fuel the imagination. And in our imagination we have to see ourselves living out the consequences of the suggestion, whether good or bad. Then we will likely either act toward it or we will react against it.* In the case of smoking, the individual who begins the habit imagines themself becoming, as a result, more popular, a part of the in-crowd, more like a particular movie star, or as a rebel against society. The countersuggestion that the individual will get sick generally doesn't capture the imagination because the very real consequences seem so far in the future. In the case of quitting smoking, the hypnotist or the autosuggestion must undo the earlier messaging and belief that smoking would be, in some way, beneficial to the individual.

Autosuggestions become part of our worldview, which we uphold with distortion, deletion, and generalization,[5] as well as minimizations and exaggerations. We do not mold our worldview consciously, of course, intending to distort, delete, or generalize to the point that our perception of reality is twisted and our relationships made more difficult. We do this unconsciously.

Distortions occur when we misinterpret actions or events. A woman who has been cheated on in romantic relationships might react with suspicion by asking her boyfriend what he feels guilty about when

---

*This, of course, is precisely why ads are populated either by happy and highly attractive individuals or by people who are more ordinary and familiar. It is natural to imagine and identify with people who are either beautiful or are like us.

he unexpectedly gives her flowers to show his appreciation for her. A corporate manager might view an especially hardworking and talented subordinate not as a loyal employee who can be counted on but, perhaps due to a situation with a previous company, as deliberately posing a challenge to their authority. Of course, while people will often see malice in innocent behavior, we also sometimes see malicious or self-serving acts as innocent. A woman might really believe that her violent boyfriend loves her and will protect her just because he cries after assaulting her. If friends or family try to get her to leave her abuser, she might even misinterpret their intentions, viewing them with suspicion.

With deletion, we expunge memories that do not support our self-defeating narrative. Someone who is struggling to stick with a healthy diet might explain, and believe, that this is because they have no willpower. Yet this same person might have quit various unwanted habits, studied extremely hard at college, and might be working long hours every day. The individual blocks all of this out, or downplays its importance, in order to sustain their self-image as someone who is powerless to resist temptation. We might be angry at a romantic partner for never doing anything nice for us, deleting all the times they gave us gifts, took us to restaurants, or surprised us in other ways. Or we might minimize their significance.

With generalizations, we turn a specific event into an alleged pattern. You've undoubtedly heard someone claim that there is no point in trying something new, such as a new job or career, because as they will say, "with my luck" it won't work out. Someone who is accidentally overcharged on a credit card might explode in a fit of anger, claiming that people are "always" trying to take advantage of them. Or a freelancer who is nervous and undercharged for their work for a few years might feel that they cannot even charge the going rate later on because "people won't pay it," which, of course, they will.

Minimizations are playing down the significance of something—usually a person's actions or words. In its more extreme form, an individual might completely deny that they are effectively being held hostage by another person (e.g., a boyfriend or girlfriend) who is threatening or abusing them in some way. They might sometimes admit what has been happening, then at other times say that they exaggerated or misunderstood the situation or that the previously reported abuse simply never happened. All of us, however, choose to register some things and not others, focusing on the positive points of a CEO's talk rather than, for example, the brief mention of cost-cutting, which might include layoffs sometime down the road.

Exaggerations are the flipside of the coin, of course. Instead of minimizing and denying, an individual might mentally zoom in on a specific action, word, or if extremely sensitive, facial expression, reading into it all kinds of intentions that the other person might not have at all. We'll look more at self-talk later on, but here we might note that we don't just misinterpret others, we also misevaluate ourselves, minimizing some of our skills or qualities and exaggerating others in our own mind so that the way we see ourselves is sometimes completely different from the way most other people perceive us.

Hypnotists have known for centuries or longer that language—what we are told and especially what we tell ourselves—shapes our perception of the world and ourselves. Our mindset has real-world consequences. As we have noted, positive suggestions from the hypnotist can overwrite the negative self-talk of the client, creating a new perception of the world and of themself. But we can also use positive self-talk to combat our own negative self-talk. When individuals have to perform a duty or do "something reasonable," according to Coué, they should "make the words *difficult, impossible, I cannot, it is stronger than I, I cannot prevent myself from* . . . disappear from [their] vocabulary," replacing them with "[it] *is easy*" and that "*I can* [do it],"[6] effectively overwriting the old beliefs and self-image with the conscious autosuggestion. According to Coué, this would not only make the task appear easier, it would actually make it easier.

You must be careful about what you say to yourself and others. Of course, sometimes unexpected events occur that require us to change our plans but, in general, make promises only if you are capable of keeping them and fully intend to keep them. If you habitually break your promises to others, knowing that your intentions and words count for little, you will find it very difficult to keep the promises you make to yourself.

People often make big promises so that they have an excuse not to do anything at all. After ten years of no physical exercise, an individual will promise himself that he will start with intense, two-hour workouts, knowing that when it's time to start there will be plenty of excuses: I don't have two hours to spare tonight; things have come up, I'll start another night; I don't have the energy for a two-hour workout tonight; I'll be aching tomorrow if I work out now and I have an important day tomorrow; I'll do it next week; and so on.

It's the same when it comes to making promises to people we care about. The person who says "I would die for you" is often the same person who won't do what matters day-to-day. The individual uses the big claim as a big excuse, thinking to themself *I would do this really big thing if it ever came to it so why should I do all these little things?*

Keeping your word matters. *Harvard Business Review* has said that "every company is a dynamic network of promises."[7] Company representatives make commitments to customers, suppliers, and staff; employees make commitments to senior staff and coworkers to perform certain tasks by a specific time so that the company is able to function as, or better than, expected. But almost every other organization or group can be said to be such a network of promises. It doesn't matter if the organization is a voluntary society with chapters across the entire globe, a group of closely bonded friends, or a network of individuals who meet periodically for some purpose (to work out, to discuss philosophy, or to make art or music). Members commit to doing certain things at certain times, or we might say they commit to a code of behavior.

Fulfilling one's promises to the organization prevents chaos from raising its ugly head. If a leader in the group cannot be trusted to keep their word, other members of the group will become dissatisfied. In response, they will usually either attempt to replace the problem leader or, more likely, they will leave the group. Unfortunately some individuals like to assert their authority, real or imagined, by doing such things as being continually late for meetings, consequently inconveniencing other members who turned up on time. This occurs in large corporations and it occurs among groups of friends. Occasionally things happen to derail a plan, of course. But when individuals continually break their promises other group members will begin to view them as unreliable and perhaps as an impediment to the success of the group.

To really be true to your word you must understand language—deeply. Most people speak with little thought or awareness of the implication of their words. We discussed language in the previous chapter and later we will explore the idea of connections. Endeavor to understand the connections between words. *Personality*, for example, is related to *person*, *persona*, and *personify*, among other terms. And while many people conflate "personality" and "character," through recourse to etymology (the history of words) we find that they represent different qualities: the inner nature and the outer face of the individual (*character* ultimately deriving from Greek *kharaktēr*, "defining quality" or an engraved or imprinted mark). All words have their connections to other words, historical and contemporary. Become conscious of these and you will more easily understand the subtexts of what other people are saying, or trying to avoid saying. Moreover, your own thinking will be clearer and your speech will become more precise and effective.

Here, I want you to start thinking about how you use your words and I want you to contemplate language itself so that you begin to understand its magic. Do you react to events ("react" implies you act without thinking) or do you respond to them ("respond" implies that you make intelligent use of your resources in regard to the situation)? Are you busy, which is a synonym for fussy and etymologically derived from the Old English word *bisig*, which can mean "anxious," or are you productive, meaning that you are producing or bringing forth the things that you conceived into the world, or being creative, acting with purpose? Do you tell yourself that life is unfair and that you cannot act to improve yourself or your situation or that you can do it, rising to any challenge? When someone asks how you're doing, is your inclination to complain about how difficult life is to try to get sympathy? Or do you focus on the positives, empowering yourself and others?

Continually contemplate your self-talk and change any words and phrases with negative or disempowering connotations for positive, empowering ones. Replace *react* with *respond*, *busy* with *productive*, and *problem* or *challenge* with *opportunity*. Hold yourself to account and make sure that you are responding not reacting, being productive not making busy work, and creating opportunities out of challenges. Always follow through with the work itself.

7
Five Roots of Personal Presence

CHARISMATIC PEOPLE HAVE PRESENCE. Often, as soon as a charismatic person walks in the room, we notice them. Even though they may not be speaking loudly or grabbing our attention with exaggerated gestures, they have a certain something that sets them apart. They seem whole.

Our word *whole* is derived from the Old English word *hal*, meaning "healthy," "unhurt," and "uninjured." Similarly, the word *holistic*, which is often associated with integrative medicine, derives from the Greek word *holos*, also meaning "whole." Today though, our lives are compartmentalized, fragmented, injured, disintegrating. They are, in other words, an embodiment of the chaos that swirls around us. Not only do we speak differently to acquaintances, friends, our romantic partner, employers, to persons of authority, and those individuals who are in no position to give us anything we want, we adopt a different demeanor toward them. Our posture is different. Our facial expressions are different. Our heart beats faster or slower. Our breath quickens or slows down. We are relaxed or tense. Our thoughts are of a different quality: embarrassed, fearful, nervous, joyful, and so on. Our vocabulary changes. We are different people, none of them fully formed and all of them reacting to circumstances.

We are going to explore the five roots of personal presence or personal charisma: the face, heart, breath, calm exterior, and posture. We will explore these partly from the perspective of symbolism and culture (especially the face) and more importantly, we will look at how to adjust each so that you return to a more natural and holistic condition in which mind and body are integrated so that you can exude presence.

Practice the technique outlined in this chapter throughout your day and in ordinary circumstances. Simply recall the technique and adjust your facial muscles, breathing, posture, and so on, so that you are able to move through your day and to interact with different people as yourself. To be clear, this doesn't mean that you will act the same in wildly different circumstances. It means that you will feel more consistent, more stable, and more authentically yourself. It means that by acting appropriately to the circumstances you will have more inner resources to draw upon. Let's begin.

THE FACE

Beyond washing, grooming, and cosmetics, rarely do we consider the face. Yet the face, inseparable from our self-image, influences our worldview, relationships, and ultimately what we can—or believe we can—achieve. In other words, how we habitually and unconsciously mold our face affects who we are and who and what we will become.

Our facial expressions keep us locked into habitual patterns of self-talk. They determine how we "face" the world, "face" the future, and "face" the unknown. In China, the art of *mian xiang* (or face reading) is supposed to be able to reveal a person's character, luck, and destiny through examining the proportions and shape of the face. Even in the West we speak of the eyes as the "window of the soul."

We adopt an expression or our faces tense up slightly, unconsciously, as we approach each new situation, as if it is the same situation that we have experienced before. This can be a useful shortcut to getting to the state of mind that we need to be in to perform at our best. But much of the time, our facial habits can be an impediment, keeping us locked into the past and locked into our own insecurities and ego. A martial arts student might screw up their face, grimacing while attempting some new technique or drill. Or an athlete might grimace when reaching the limits of their strength. That grimace might signal to the consciousness that now is the time for sacrificing all of one's energy and willpower to the task at hand in one last explosion of energy. More likely, it will signal to the consciousness that the task is too complicated or physically challenging for the individual to perform.

Molding our face begins early in life. As children we learn to respond to threatening situations—the criticism of a teacher, the anger of a parent, or the mocking laughter of other children—by masking our fear and embarrassment, unconsciously molding a facial expression that becomes reflexive and automatic. We have probably all seen small children grinning when they are being reprimanded, and you might remember forcing this facial expression as a child when you were chastised or punished and felt threatened or embarrassed.

Later in life, a stressful job, environment, or relationship will reinforce the defensiveness of the face. Whenever we encounter—or face—a possible threat or situation that might make us uncomfortable, muscle memory kicks in and our face switches, without us even being aware, to the default facial mask that we created for our own emotional protection. Sometimes our reactive facial expression is subtle: a slight knitting of the brow; an almost imperceptible tension around the eye sockets; raised eyebrows; or a nervous smile. Sometimes it is obvious.

Facial expressions aren't simply physical reflections of our emotions and thoughts; they also influence them. In other words, there is a feedback loop. An individual begins to feel a certain emotion such as fear, automatically makes the associated facial expression, and the facial expression reinforces the belief that the individual is right to experience the emotion at that moment in time. Actors mimic experiencing emotions and in making the facial expressions of happiness, pain, grief, anger, and so on, they begin to actually feel these emotions.

Studies have shown that women who get Botox injections to reduce the appearance of glabellar wrinkles, which run horizontally across the faces of many people as they age, are often happier as a result. Of course, feeling better about how we look might be enough to make us feel a little happier. But Botox works by numbing the muscles in the forehead, rendering the patient unable to frown and make facial expressions associated with stress, worry, and anger (but still able to smile) for several months at a time. It is this prolonged inability to make facial expressions of negative emotions that appears to make Botox act "as a mood elevator" for many people.[1]

But there is also a cultural component. Different cultures have conceived of the human face in different ways and it has had a different status in the fine arts. In China and Japan, the landscape was more important and the portrait was of little interest. In the latter country, when an artist created a portrait it was highly stylized and bore little resemblance to the real-life individual. Conversely, in Europe the portrait was considered to be the highest form of painting, superior to the landscape and far superior to still life.

On ancient coins, the face of the king or emperor was stamped. The ruler's face signified authority. It guaranteed—even to some extent created—the worth of the coin. In later European portrait paintings we see the sitter, often in a three-quarter profile, gazing into the distance, lost in thought, or perhaps looking at us. They are relaxed and confident. Rarely is there even a hint of a smile.

Almost by definition, a portrait depicts an authority: a king, queen, prince, duke, duchess, or a religious figure such as a saint. Their job is not to please or appease us but to show us what authority—temporal, spiritual, intellectual—is like. We need to see this. A temporal authority such as a king might be called to "face" an enemy in battle. He will have to "face" the challenges of his society. At times, he will need to "face the facts" and, at other times, he will "face" uncertainty.

Yet despite their differences, most cultures have a concept of the face. Today we speak of the "game face" and the "face off." The former refers to the facial expression adopted by an individual as part of the mental preparation for facing an approaching challenging situation (originally an athlete before a contest). The latter refers to a confrontation between two individuals or teams. We talk of "saving face," meaning to do something to save one's reputation, and in China there is the concept of "giving face," meaning to show respect to someone in public. Again, a person who is too modest and never claims any credit for their achievements is said to be self-effacing (*efface* means "to remove the face").

When we see traditional paintings or sculptures of the Buddha, Jesus, Krishna, or saints, their expressions are usually serene. Except perhaps for a faint smile, their facial muscles appear to be totally relaxed and they are free of both the laughter lines and stress lines that inevitably emerge over time as we engage the world. Often there is an aliveness to the eyes of these spiritual exemplars. At other times though, the eyes are closed and it is almost as if they are asleep. Yet, these are the faces of the "awakened"* who see reality as it actually is.

In the modern era, we have almost lost touch with the face and, rather than it expressing our inner authority and our own individuality, we use it as a mask. The conformity of the face begins in childhood. In the company of strangers, friends, or relatives, our parents will instruct their children to smile whenever they are feeling sad or angry; they will also insist on the child smiling for photographs.

This habit becomes ingrained. Instead of laughing at danger, an individual learns to smile at the angry parent, the overbearing boss, or the threatening stranger on the street—smiling fawningly in the vain hope that this will dissolve the threat. The photographs of most adults show people looking directly into the camera with a staged smile. It doesn't matter the context or background of the photo; the same expression is there in every situation as if the individual is no more than a

---

**Buddha* derives from the Pali *budh*, meaning "to awaken," "to know," or "to perceive," and from Sanskrit *bodhati*, "awake," "observe," or "understand."

cardboard cutout, a prop moved from place to place. The backdrop changes but the expression remains fixed.

In group photos, too, we often see everyone in the same posture, staring at the camera with the same expression. And on social media we also see attractive young women getting the same minor cosmetic surgery (especially lip fillers) as every other attractive female influencer. Their different faces begin to morph into the same face. This is not a societally idealized face per se. Rather, it is a kind of symbolic face. The surgically filled lips, out of proportion to the rest of the face. are meant to signify high status, luxury, and wealth—a woman who is out of reach of the average man but who can be fantasized about. The obviousness of the surgery may detract from the woman's beauty but it fits with the backdrop of rented yachts, rented luxury apartments, and island beaches. The public face (the persona or mask) starts to become more important than the real person.

More common is the face of stress. Indeed, the fawning smile of the employee to the boss disguises stress, insecurity, and fear of the future. In the average individual, tension builds up in the face. One might frown habitually, knot the brow, clench the jaw, or grind the teeth, sometimes causing considerable pain and even damage to the teeth and jaw. Perhaps because we are so cerebral and so out of touch with our bodies and our hearts, our tension and fear become lodged in the face and throat; hence the expression "my heart was in my throat," meaning that the speaker felt afraid. Even the voice will become higher in pitch as we become accustomed to all of our feelings being in the face and neck, and speak from the neck rather than the chest.

For good or ill, our facial expression not only represents but subtly shapes or reinforces our mindset. It shows everyone, and it shows us, how we "face the world."

As you move through your day, mentally monitor your face for any tension. And wherever you notice tension, allow that area to relax. To encourage relaxation, mentally tell yourself that the area of tension is relaxing: think to yourself *my forehead is relaxing*, or *my jaw is relax-*

ing. The point here is not to develop a sagging, hanging, lethargic, and empty expression, but to use effort efficiently. To return the face to a natural state (a natural state means poise) keep the lips closed, with the tongue touching the roof of the mouth just behind the teeth, but do not clench or strain the jaw muscles.

At first it may be difficult to notice even quite severe tension as we form our facial expressions habitually and unconsciously and simply come to accept the tension in our face as "normal." If you have lines in a certain area of your face, such as on the forehead or around the eyes, this is a sign that you are tensing that area most of all, so you can begin by relaxing it. However, even if you are tensing in one area, it is almost certain that you are tensing elsewhere and that these different areas of tension are connected. If you are tensing the forehead, for example, you might notice that it automatically relaxes once you relax the jaw or chin and vice versa.

Tension in the face has an upward and inward motion. When we clench our jaw, we push the lower jaw up into the upper jaw. We push the chin up. We squint, pushing the orbicularis oculi muscles (below the eyes) upward. And we raise our eyebrows, frowning. In regard to the inward motion, we will knit our brows and purse our lips. Recognizing this, you can also begin by reversing these directions. Allow the eyebrows to lower slightly. Allow the muscles around and below the eyes to relax. Allow the lips to relax so that they do not feel tight. Allow the chin to lower slightly. Keeping the lips together, allow the jaw to lower slightly as well. To make it easier, as you work down through your face, mentally tell yourself that each area is relaxing (*my forehead is relaxing, my brow is relaxing*, and so on).

Because our habitual facial expressions have been formed over many years, you will almost certainly notice that the muscles soon want to tense up again. When you notice this, just allow that area to relax as before. Over time you will notice more and more subtle layers of tension, but you will also be able to relax your face for longer periods and you will be able to return your face to a more relaxed state much quicker.

THE HEART

Different cultures in different times and places have associated the heart with mysterious power. The ancient Egyptians said that the god Ptah had first conceived the universe in his heart.[2] In Catholicism, since the late seventeenth century a feast or "solemnity" of the Sacred Heart of Jesus has been held every year on the Friday following the second Sunday after Pentecost. Sufism is often called "the way of the heart." And in ancient Norse mythology, when the hero Sigurd tastes a drop of blood from the heart of the dragon Fafnir, he is able to understand the language of the birds, meaning he gained supernatural insight.

Today of course, we explicitly associate the heart with feelings of romantic love, of which it is the most common symbol. Certainly this organ does seem to be linked to what and who we desire. For several decades there have been occasional reports of the personalities of heart transplant patients changing in significant ways after this surgery. Changes in preferences for certain food, music, and art have been noted; on rare occasions changes in sexuality have been perceived. A range of explanations have been offered, including the effects of drugs or stress associated with the surgery. However, these sometimes dramatic changes often reflect the personality or tastes of the donor, whom the recipient did not know.[3]

Paul Pearsall, Gary Schwartz, and Linda Russek have provided multiple examples of patients who had received a new heart, seemingly spontaneously having the same impulses as their heart donor. In one case, an eighteen-year-old woman was given the heart of an eighteen-year-old man. He played the guitar and wrote poetry. Although the female patient had no interest in music before her heart transplant—and not knowing anything of her donor—she suddenly became interested in music and began to learn to play the guitar.[4] Another woman who had always loved eating meat received the heart of a vegetarian. After the surgery, she found that she was suddenly repulsed by the idea of eating meat and became a vegetarian.[5]

As we have said already, due to our tendency to intellectualize and our estrangement from our own hearts, our tension is often projected upward, lodging in our face. This estrangement may be especially the case with men. "A spiritual man may love light, and yet be entirely numb in the chest area," says Robert Bly in *Iron John*. Again, he says that a man's "chest feels hollow at each of his weaknesses." Prior to the modern age, work was more physical: hunting, farming, building, soldiering, or child-rearing, weaving, and so on. The body was actively engaged in the work. An individual sensed when something was right or when it was wrong by how they felt physically. The person used muscle memory. The individual used their breath—breathing deeper and harder in those moments of physical exertion—and, as such, was rooted in the chest.

We have talked of relaxing the face. Once you are used to this, relax your face, neck, and shoulders. Exhale and allow your shoulders to sink down slightly. Visualize any tension passing down the body into the ground. At the same time, visualize your center of gravity (your *gravitas*, literally Latin for "weight" and "presence") passing down from the face to the center of the chest. As you relax your shoulders, it will be easier for you to visualize your chest being weighted by your presence. Whenever you are relaxing or are out walking, relax your face and feel that gravity, gravitas, or weightiness of your presence in your chest, even as you remain mindful of your surroundings.

BREATH

There has long been the idea that the breath is connected to the sacred. The ancient Greeks word *pneuma* means "breath" and "spirit" or "soul." Similarly, the Sanskrit term *prana* and the Chinese term *chi* mean both "vital energy" and "breath." According to the Vedas, the sacred books of Hinduism, when the god Vishnu exhales, thousands of universes appear from his breath, and when he inhales those same universes are drawn back into the god.

Our breathing is, of course, directly related to our emotional state and physical condition. Breathing fast, for example, is usually a sign of physical exertion or overexertion, or fear or panic. Deep, slow breathing is generally a sign of feeling calm. Today, most people breathe in a way that is shallow. Typically this means allowing only the rib cage to move as the individual inhales and exhales. If a person has practiced meditation, however, they will often breathe into their stomach instead, not moving the ribs at all. Often this is mistaken for deep breathing.

Instead, as you relax your face and feel your center of gravity lower into your chest, breathe slowly and deeply, into both your chest and your stomach. As you inhale, allow both your chest and your stomach to expand. Do not strain your lungs or force yourself to breathe longer or deeper than is comfortable. Your breathing should feel natural and pleasant and should be calming.

To get used to this, you can practice first expanding your chest and then, as you continue to breathe, expanding your stomach. Or imagine that you are breathing through your solar plexus and that the air is going up into the chest and down into the stomach at the same time.

This way of breathing will help you to feel calm and it will also help others to feel relaxed around you. Typically we prefer people who make us feel calm to those who make us feel nervous, or who seem stressed, overly energized, or erratic.

CALM EXTERIOR

We tend to associate power with muscular tension, brute strength, gritted teeth, bodily rigidity, and a stern and uncompromising demeanor. Yet power comes partly from relaxation. In martial arts, the force and effectiveness of a punch come from its speed: the greater the speed, the greater the force it will have. Tensing the muscles of the arm only stiffens the arm and slows down the strike. Instead, the martial artist has to learn to relax the arm as they punch, tensing only when the fist is an inch or so away from the target. We can apply this principle to much of life.

The early psychoanalyst Wilhelm Reich noticed that his patients would willingly talk about their problems but would resist making necessary lifestyle changes in order to overcome them. Reich believed that this "rigid responsiveness" was a defense mechanism used to protect the individual from "unacceptable feelings" as well as from outside threats, at least in the subconscious processes of the patient. Reich also believed that muscular tension and bodily rigidity served the same function, freezing the emotions.[6] A person who is physically, mentally, or emotionally tense or rigid has locked themselves into certain patterns of thinking and behaving. We have already spoken of this in relation to the face.

There is some indication that in heterosexual relationships, women are attracted most to calm men. In a two-part study, a team at the University of Abertay Dundee, Scotland, led by Fhionna Moore, selected thirty-nine male students at the same university and measured their levels of testosterone (the so-called "male hormone") and cortisol (the "stress hormone"). In the first part of the study, forty-two women from a different university were then shown the photographs of the male subjects and, based on the photographs alone, asked to rate them for attractiveness. The men with lower cortisol levels were generally rated as more attractive while testosterone levels bore no relationship to attractiveness. High cortisol is, of course, associated with stress, whereas low cortisol is associated with being calm. And high levels of cortisol can also negatively affect health.

In the second part of the study, four composite portraits were created, with each composite being derived from men with specific testosterone and cortisol qualities: (1) high-testosterone and high-cortisol, (2) high-testosterone and low-cortisol, (3) low-testosterone and high-cortisol, (4) low-testosterone and low-cortisol. This time, forty-three women were shown the composites throughout their menstrual cycle. When the women were outside of the fertile phase of their cycle, they preferred men with either high testosterone and high cortisol or low testosterone and low cortisol, but not high in one hormone and low in the other. During the fertile phase (and thus more likely to become pregnant), however, the women found men with low cortisol more attractive. It may be that women select men with lower cortisol levels since this can indicate better health and a greater ability to remain calm under pressure; traits that would not only be desirable in a long-term relationship but that would be desirable to pass on to their children.[7]

Of course, as is suggested by the attraction of some women (outside of the fertile phase of the menstrual cycle) to men with high testosterone and high cortisol levels, calm is not the only attractive quality. We are attracted to people who appear happy, outgoing, vivacious, confident, and so on, although these, too, may be traits of low cortisol.

Nevertheless, we all prefer being around people who are calm to being around people who are stressed, and who will consequently make us or other people stressed. Indeed we admire people who are able to remain cool, calm, and collected. Especially when combined with an ability to focus on the other person by really listening to what they say, making eye contact, and engaging them in meaningful conversation, a calm demeanor is highly attractive both in regard to romantic and sexual relationships and in relation to other, nonromantic, nonsexual relationships like friendships and business relationships. In a world in which stress is normal but unwanted, a calm, relaxed, confident demeanor can make other people feel calmer and more confident, which is generally how people want to feel. Remaining calm under pressure is not only a benefit to the individual but is soft power in relation to others.

POSTURE

"To be a warrior, look like a warrior and stand like a warrior," says the famed samurai Miyamoto Musashi in *Musashi's Book of Five Rings*. "How often have you witnessed so-called experts with no form or balance?" asks Musashi, rhetorically. "You see them as clods with no style or grace."[8] We associate posture with attitude and personality, or more accurately, we regard posture as physically representing an individual's character. As such, it is no coincidence that the word *upright* means both to be physically upright, with a good posture whether standing or sitting, and morally upright, meaning honorable, conscientious, and honest. When we think of an upright person, morally speaking, we do not imagine them slouching.

In England less than a century ago, "chin up" was a common refrain. This phrase was a kind of shorthand, used to advise someone not be pessimistic or dwell on problems and to embody and give the appearance of being emotionally well-balanced. In its most literal interpretation, the expression meant that an individual should raise their head up so that it wasn't drooping. But the posture, especially for men, was also supposed to be upright with shoulders back slightly and diaphragm raised (or "chest out"). If a young man didn't stand or sit in such a way, he might well have found himself corrected by an older gentleman.

We find the upright posture integrated into clothing. In England (the home of Savile Row, synonymous with bespoke tailoring), the suit was the traditional dress for a gentleman. Notably, the traditional gentleman's suit was and still is designed to hold the body upright. The sleeves have a slight curve to fit the arms held relaxed by the wearer's sides, and multiple pieces of fabric and types of stitching inside the chest, holding it and the shoulders in place. Similarly in Japan, traditionally women wore a thick obi (sash) around the waist, which held the torso upright even when bowing.

This might seem old-fashioned but a recent study has shown that participants with an upright posture reported having a "better mood," less fear, and "higher self-esteem" than participants whose posture was slumped. Notably, too, the latter group used more words associated with negative emotions, fewer words associated with positive emotions, and more first-person singular pronouns (I, me, mine, myself).[9]

The upright posture of traditional English or Japanese dress is also the posture of someone in meditation: chin parallel to the ground, head back slightly and resting on the neck, torso upright, diaphragm raised slightly, and shoulders back. This is not a coincidence. This posture can be held unconsciously. It enables the lungs to fully expand and contract without straining. And it facilitates the mind letting go of "me" along with everything that "I" am stuck on emotionally.

Now that you have relaxed your facial muscles and your shoulders, have lowered your sense of your center of gravity to your chest, have begun to breathe in a more relaxed and deeper way, and are experiencing relaxation, adjust your posture: Lift your diaphragm a little and pull your shoulders back slightly. Make sure your chin is parallel to the ground and draw the head back slightly so that it is able to rest on your neck. Do not stiffen up. This posture should be comfortable enough to hold without conscious effort.

8
Chaos Revisited
Strangeness and Authority

WE SPOKE OF CHAOS at the beginning of this book. And strangeness—a sense of alienness, even a sense of otherworldliness—is a quality of chaos, randomness, chance, or entropy. Authority is, in a sense, it's opposite. An authoritative person is able to take charge in times of upheaval, restoring calm or faith and getting people to act rationally or to work together to solve a problem.

Earlier we looked at hypnotism briefly as well. Hypnotism—or hypnotic persuasion—can work without trance. In this case, besides the skillful use of language, it relies on two elements—authority and strangeness—to be effective. As we shall see, although we rarely think of these two qualities, especially together, they are integral to human society. Indeed, most of us use them at various points in our lives to create a positive impression, although we generally do so unconsciously.

It is important to recognize that authority is sometimes cultivated over a long period of time, while at other times it can be immediately suggested. If an army general with a chest full of medals walks into the room with his head high, we feel the pressure not to slouch. As we alluded to earlier, men often sit up straighter when a beautiful woman has walked in the room as well. This isn't simply attraction; though that is a large part of what is going on in the latter case, it is also that the woman is perceived as having high status (someone who will not settle for the average or below average).

If it is cultivated over time, as is the case with consumer brands, then the individual, group, or corporation will need to be consistent with its image, message, and quality of work. Bad decisions and stupid remarks made in public will undermine or destroy reputation and consequently authority. We spoke about asabiyyah (group loyalty) at the beginning of this book. Companies and brands also cultivate asabiyyah, in the sense of identity that people like "us" buy this product and people that are not like us do not. In recent years, some brands have criticized their own customer base or promoted another seemingly antagonistic to it and unsurprisingly have seen their profits tank. Serious financial loss should have been predictable. Strangeness or uniqueness, too, is easily lost by abandoning one's vision and trying to become popular or more like everyone else.

If authority and strangeness can be presented in the moment, without needing to cultivate them over a period of time, these hypnotic qualities rely largely on appearance and on the use of language either to persuade or to turn the target's worldview on its head. Early in this book, we noted that Dr. William Wesley Cook believed that the first quality of the successful hypnotist was "a strong and vigorous physique" that would exert a "great influence" over those whose physique was less impressive.[1] We have also looked at posture, facial expression, breathing, and other elements of personal charisma. Clothing also matters, of course. While they may occasionally inspire resentment, for the overwhelming majority, the sight of a physically attractive, stylish, and confident person enables individuals to daydream about a different and more exciting way of living. Occasionally it will spur us to take action to improve ourselves in ways that we suddenly recognize are necessary.

In his hypnotherapy practice, Milton Erickson often used language alone to help his patients to change. When he was with his patients, he would present himself as a person who had insight into the person's situation—an authority. He would also make statements that were counterintuitive and even the opposite of what the patient had heard from other therapists before—strangeness.

On one occasion, a child psychiatrist brought a defiant teenage patient named Ed to see him. The child psychiatrist expected Erickson to hypnotize the boy, but instead he simply mentioned that he had been told about his getting into trouble. Then he said to the boy, "I really don't know how you are going to change your behavior."[2] The child psychiatrist was mystified but soon the boy began to improve himself.

Erickson's statement might have implied that the boy would change; if we subtract the first part of his statement, we are—or rather the boy was—left with the suggestion that "you are going to change your behavior." His statement left the exact method of change up to the boy himself, befitting his tendency to go against authority.[3] But perhaps more importantly, although the statement implied that it would be necessary for the boy to change, Erickson *did not explain why* he should.

Undoubtedly the boy's parents and previous psychiatrists had told him why he should make an effort to improve his behavior. No doubt they had explained quite logically that if he continued to misbehave, he would get into trouble. They might have told him, too, that he would not make the right kind of friends, would not get a good job, and that he might even end up in prison. And all of this might have been accurate. But as marketing genius Rory Sutherland reminds us, "The problem with logic is that it kills off magic."[4] By magic, Sutherland does not mean the occult; he means surprise, wonder, the unexpected, the counterintuitive, what captures our imagination, or what we are calling "strangeness" and what Sutherland also calls "illogic." He is quite correct. Mystery, the unexplained, and by extension, the absence of explanation, all create authority.

Erickson might have suggested that he did not know how the boy would effect a change in himself, but he also implied, subtly but strongly, that he was intimate with this other way of being and by extension, another world or way of life that was out of reach to an unruly teenage boy. He was the authority. And as an authority, Erickson did not need to explain himself—indeed he should not have explained himself since that would only imply that he was more or less on the same level as the child.

With difficult adult patients, in contrast to their previous psychiatrists, Erickson would not argue with them or tell them that they had to get better. He would simply listen to them. And to their surprise, he would even express agreement with them. If they said they could not be hypnotized, for example, instead of insisting that they could be, Erickson would say that they were perhaps correct. Then he would go further, adding something like, "you may not ever be able to experience the comfort and pleasure of hypnosis."[5] Agreeing when everyone has disagreed introduces strangeness. But by telling the patient that they might never know how good it feels to be hypnotized he is also making himself the authority. Erickson knows. The stubborn client does not—and the client has been stubborn because they have seen themself as the person who knows more.

AUTHORITY AND STRANGENESS IN SOCIETY

Unsurprisingly perhaps, Ericksonian hypnotherapy provided the foundation for neuro-linguistic programming and influenced the world of sales and marketing. Nevertheless, leaving formal hypnotism aside, lying behind creativity and the acceptance of new ideas and technology, or "consumerism," are the twin forces of strangeness and authority. As such, they are integral to any society that is dynamic enough to respond to evolving challenges.

In the consumer market, strangeness means novelty or newness—new products and potential new experiences for the consumer. At its best, a new product or consumer experience is what Seth Godin calls a "purple cow." It is something interesting and exceptional; something that grabs our attention when other—perhaps similar—things have become invisible to us through familiarity (brown cows).[6] Of course, we are generally wary of the unknown and the unfamiliar, and the vast majority of people do not want to be seen doing something different than everyone else. Subcultures may oppose the mainstream, but within their group, members will try to conform to each other as much as possible. For new things to be accepted then, the creator or producer must have authority. Regardless of whether the creator or producer is an individual, a small collective, or a large corporation, authority is created to varying degrees through branding, or the conscious creation and cultivation of a brand image.

Sociologist and communication theorist Everett Rogers categorizes the adopters of innovations into five different types of consumers: (1) innovators, (2) early adopters, (3) early majority, (4) late majority, and (5) laggards.

"Innovators are active information seekers about new ideas," says Rogers. They avidly consume mass media and their "interpersonal networks extend over a wide area."[7] They are also "cosmopolites." Students at an art college might adopt an innovative style of dress, for example, because the authorities they look to are experimenters in culture (Andy Warhol in fine art or Alexander McQueen in fashion). Such innovators are not looking to adopt something wholesale but, rather, are interested in new ideas.

Early adopters are the first segment of mainstream society to buy into the emerging trend. For them, the innovators are the authority. By the time we reach laggards, we are talking about those who merely want to keep up with the rest of society. They are the most localite and often have small social circles of friends and acquaintances and frequently, too, these circles are largely composed of individuals with more traditional values. For them, the majority and what has become the status quo constitute the authority.[8]

One of the most notable classes of authority in our society is the celebrity: actors, singers, musicians, comedians, and so on. This includes celebrities and celebutantes—the latter being celebrities who are "famous for being famous." Among the celebutante set we find Paris Hilton and Kim Kardashian. Notably, while most celebutantes cannot—to the best of the public's knowledge—sing, dance, act, or do any of the things that celebrities normally do, they are usually highly physically attractive and have or create an air of glamor about them by being seen at celebrity events, wearing designer clothing, and so on. And regardless of their lack of apparent talent, celebutantes also sometimes eventually appear in various TV shows, ads, and occasionally movies. While celebutantes usually attract attention for their looks and lifestyle, we should not write them off as unintelligent. They are usually adept at understanding how fame works and what the public wants to see.

The celebutante radicalizes Dr. William Wesley Cook's first law of the successful hypnotist (to exude health and physical presence) by being the most beautiful, tantalizing, desirable, and glamorous of the celebrity elite. By being an innovator of style a celebrity or celebutante shows that he or—more often—she is not only distinctly different from ordinary society but an insider and an authority on the world of fame. A celebrity may endorse a fashion brand (usually being loaned or given expensive clothing for free) but the brand also endorses the celebrity. The relationship is mutually reinforcing of each other's celebrity status.

Like celebrities and other movers and shakers of society, celebutantes often seem to appear out of nowhere. And the enigmatic stranger with no known past has long been entrancing to their host nation. Knowing nothing about their earlier life and little about their culture, we willingly project our fantasies onto the stranger, seeing them as more spiritual, more intelligent, and wiser or perhaps, in contrast, more connected, more glamorous, freer, and more in control and able to navigate the chaos of the world.

By default, the stranger with a different worldview or mission brings both an air of mystery (strangeness) and an air of authority; hence, the missionary. Leaving aside mainstream religions and such internationally known figures as the current Dalai Lama, many lesser known but influential spiritual teachers have been most active far outside of their home countries during the modern era. The Russian emigre Mme. Helena

Blavatsky founded the Theosophical movement in New York City. The Greek Armenian G. I. Gurdjieff was active in Paris and Russia. The Canadian Manly P. Hall was active in Los Angeles and is still best known in the United States. The Indian guru Swami Vivekenanda promoted Hindu spirituality in America during the nineteenth century. And during the twentieth and early twenty-first centuries, a number of Indian spiritual gurus, tantric gurus, and yoga gurus have dazzled the upper and middle classes of the United States, sometimes only to leave behind a very mixed reputation later on.

Other classes of strangers include law enforcement officers and criminals. We wonder why grown men occasionally confess to a crime that they did not commit. Our perception of police interrogations, after all, is that it is something like a Socratic dialogue. We imagine the investigating officers probing the suspect and through a series of questions and answers, arriving at the truth. Instead police interrogations (which can last for hours) employ exactly the qualities of authority and strangeness: the authority of the interrogating police and the strangeness of the situation and of what the police say. In regard to the last of these, an investigating officer might appear angry when the suspect asserts their innocence but might speak softly, smile, and reassure the suspect that they will do everything they can to help if the suspect confesses to the crime. Such behavior is contrary to everything we have experienced and thought normal throughout our lives and combined with authority it is—or can be—hypnotic. Irrational situations sometimes solicit irrational responses—false confessions being one of them.

Criminals—especially con men—use strangeness and authority as well to commit some crimes. To create a false sense of authority, a criminal might flash a fake ID. Or more simply but effectively, he might dress smartly and professionally. He will also be well-groomed, of course, and try to affect an upright posture that suggests confidence.

About two years after I moved from London to New York City, while still in something of a honeymoon period with the city, I was almost robbed. But the technique used was highly unusual, confusing, and even hypnotic. It was the middle of the day and I was in a busy area of midtown Manhattan, standing and looking around for a specific address. I noticed a man in his early twenties about thirty feet away, walking toward me. He was about six foot two and so easily visible even in the crowd. He was also impeccably dressed in a sports jacket and chinos and well groomed. I noticed something was strange, however, as he locked eyes with me.

As he was about to walk past me he suddenly veered off course, bashing into my left shoulder and arm. I turned around, expecting him to threaten me verbally since he had deliberately walked into me when I was standing still. Instead, in a very soft voice with a placid and very polite tone, he said, "Excuse me, but you just walked into me and you broke my glasses." He showed me a pair of glasses that he had been holding in his left hand. Then he began to tell me that he was a student and that he needed them for his college work and he couldn't afford new glasses. "If you give me a hundred dollars, I'll be happy with that," he said. If I didn't have a hundred dollars on me we could go to a cash machine, he suggested, again very softly and politely. Yet at the same time, he was also physically up close to me, leaning into me a little—a posture that was subtly menacing.

Not entirely acclimatized to my new city and its rules of behavior, I was confused by what was going on. However, probably less than a minute into the robbery attempt, the would-be robber's less patient and lower-IQ accomplice appeared. Scruffy, stocky, angry looking, and a cliche of a criminal, he addressed the smartly dressed would-be robber, saying, "What's the hold up?" (meaning, why was the ruse taking so long). If the ruse had worked I would either have handed a hundred dollars to the robber or I would have gone to a cash machine, where I have no doubt I would have found a knife pulled on me with a demand for far more cash. With the appearance of robber number two and his plain talking, the spell was broken and I promptly left the scene. Let's list the indicators of authority that the first would-be robber was using:

- Eye contact
- A smartly dressed and well-groomed appearance
- Certainty in his use of language, insisting that I had broken his glasses when this obviously wasn't the case
- The claim that he was a student, generally regarded as people who are trying to get on in life through their own hard work
- A calm voice with no indication of stress
- A domineering posture (not advisable in most situations)

Now let's consider the contradictions (strangeness) used in this robbery attempt:

- The first robber was dressed very smartly but claimed he was a student and couldn't afford new glasses.
- He said that I had walked into him, but I had been standing still and he had walked into me.
- His words were polite and he spoke softly, but his physical posture was threatening.
- Again, his words were polite and softly spoken but his statement, "If you give me a hundred dollars, I'll be happy with that," implies a threat: that he would be unhappy if I did not give him the money, and his being unhappy would be bound to have some unpleasant consequences.

Through the contradictory use of language and behavior, and contradictory behavior and dress, the first robber doubtlessly fully intended to create confusion—and compliance—in his would-be victims. I might have only been there for a minute, in a state of confusion, but from a self-defense perspective that was a minute too long.

Now let's turn to romantic and sexual relationships. Fantasizing about having sex with a stranger—real or imagined—is extremely common among both men and women.[9] And fantasizing specifically about foreigners, romantically, is far from unusual.[10] Imagining sex in an unusual location is also common. Indeed, almost by definition, sexual fantasy involves the unusual (to the person doing the fantasizing). Authority creeps into sexual fantasies as well, of course, with thoughts of being dominated sexually or imagining having sex with a celebrity or authority figure.[11]

We will often try to introduce strangeness into our own romantic relationships, usually to impress the other person. We might take our date to an unfamiliar, upscale restaurant or somewhere else that is beautiful that they have not been to before, and there we will try to present ourselves as someone of authority, telling them about the best aspects of our lives, our accomplishments, our overcoming of some struggles, and so on. Of course, some individuals will undoubtedly take a date somewhere familiar, such as an inexpensive fast-food restaurant, but such an ordinary experience will likely summon up only ordinary feelings, making a second date far less likely.

While going for a walk through nature or visiting a museum are fairly typical dates, we must note that watching a horror movie together is also a fairly common—if counterintuitive—date. Since the plots of horror movies generally involve death, murder, hauntings, possessions, and malevolent supernatural phenomena, such movies seem entirely incongruous with romance. However, as with virtually everything else in our lives, dating isn't a matter of logic. Horror movies cause arousal in their viewers. Epinephrine spikes. The heart rate increases. The pupils dilate. And we might begin to sweat a little bit. How we experience such arousal is largely determined by the conscious mind, which will interpret it as fear, excitement, or sexual desire. As such, the arousal caused by a horror movie can be and often is "relabeled" as sexual attraction by those watching one during a romantic date.[12]

However, since it is undeniable that horror movies embody the quality of strangeness to probably the maximum degree possible for the average human being, we do not really need to go into body mechanics and psychology. Strangeness causes arousal. It takes us out of our ordinary world and the restrictions placed on us by convention, and more importantly, it relieves us of the limits that we have placed on our own actions.

While the plots of many horror movies may be ridiculous, it would be difficult to think of any other contemporary form of entertainment that plunges the consumer into a world so different from our own. While watching such a movie with a romantic partner, authority might be expressed by not flinching and not exhibiting fear. The relabeling of fear as sexual desire is doubtlessly often helped along by the reassuring holding of hands at the most gruesome moments.

There are differences between the aforementioned circumstances and uses and effects of authority and strangeness, of course. In threatening situations, the latter quality is often manifested as a contradiction, especially the combination of threat and reassurance, and is used to confuse and intimidate so that the victim won't know how, or even whether, to react. In positive experiences such as a romantic date, strangeness usually takes the form of an unfamiliar aesthetic experience like a beautiful restaurant, nature at sunset, a horror movie, or for weddings, an elaborately decorated place of worship, a castle, or sandy beach in the Bahamas, and is used to create a sense of wonder, excitement, awe, meaning, or destiny.

9
The Six Cs
A Survival Guide for a Time of AI

WE BEGAN THIS BOOK by looking at chaos. Chance, randomness, and providence play their parts, sometimes bringing "good fortune," sometimes bringing "bad luck." What matters is how we respond to challenges and whether we can turn short-term setbacks into long-term success.

Emerging artificial intelligence (AI) threatens to create greater chaos than we have seen in decades, replacing many of the more intelligent individuals in our societies just as advances in machinery destroyed many skilled jobs decades ago. Over the last century, education in Western countries has become increasingly focused on standardized testing, and as such, has emphasized intelligence and memorization. Though highly valuable, these qualities will not be enough to compete in a world integrated with AI.

Although common to classical cultures (ancient Greece, Confucian China, and the Islamic Middle East and Persia), completely missing from our modern conception of education and of individuality itself is the notion of the whole person who should develop themselves mentally, physically, spiritually, culturally, ethically, and behaviorally. Of course, we find math, sport, and music all taught at schools, but the underlying assumption is that some children will develop in one area and others in another area, with some growing up to become accountants and others musicians, for example.

Despite what is often imagined, top U.S. colleges and probably those in most of the world prefer students who are exceptional at one thing to students who score high across the board.[1] On the mass level, Western education has produced unbalanced, fragmented individuals who associate only with people with the same interests and opinions and consequently have enormous blind spots in their view of the world and serious limitations in regard to their creative capacity. Nevertheless, this focus on the exceptional at the college level has helped to foster geniuses who are sooner or later able to make major breakthroughs, either in their field or in another, though often not the one they initially trained in.

Nevertheless, as we begin to understand human biology to a greater degree than ever before, and as we face challenges from artificial intelligence, significant segments of society will recognize that developing ourselves as a whole will confer major advantages in the future. Indeed, we will want to develop ourselves as a whole if for no other reason than it will enable us to develop our thinking and to make novel connections. But we should not ignore the benefits of health nor of the authority that comes with a healthy body, looks, good posture, and persuasive use of language.

This chapter is a guide for surviving and thriving in a time of chaos, uncertainty, unpredictability, and change, which we are now entering with the emergence of AI and will be living through for the coming decades. For many people, AI already appears unbeatable. And unsurprisingly so. Goldman Sachs has predicted that 300 million jobs will be "disrupted" worldwide by 2030.[2] Adaptability, out-of-the-box thinking, creativity, and the right mindset will be needed to survive and to thrive over the coming decades. We will explore this soon.

AI is already producing art, music, photographic-like images, realistic videos, and more, seemingly from little more than a few "prompts." It is, of course, also aiding researchers in every field from medicine to archaeology, economics, and political campaigning. Hundreds of millions of people are also turning to AI programs for advice. Yet, far from the unbiased, super-rational machine-brain that it is presented as, whether intentionally or not, AI is often trained to regurgitate the biases of its trainers. Or it can be trained on biased data, which inevitably skews any kind of results that it produces. Either way, AI systems can have significant blind spots and vulnerabilities built into them. And users of AI often adopt these biases.[3]

In 2016, Google's AlphaGo beat the Go world champion, Lee Sedol, in four out of five games of the Chinese game of strategy.[4] Six years after AlphaGo had beaten Sedol, in 2022, a research team led by MIT Ph.D. student Tony T. Wang pitted amateur players against KataGo, "the strongest publicly available Go-playing AI system" at that time. It should have been a bloodbath with KataGo defeating the amateurs almost as soon as the games had begun. But the research team had discovered, and were able to exploit, a simple vulnerability in the AI system, which led to the amateurs winning virtually every game. "Even in KataGo agents adversarially trained to defend against [the research team's] attack," it was still more or less defenseless against the amateurs. At the end of the study, the team showed that,

> Using less than 14% of the computer used to train KataGo, we obtain adversarial policies that win >99% of the time against KataGo with no search, and >97% of the time against KataGo with enough search to be superhuman. Critically, our adversaries do not win by playing Go well. Instead, they trick KataGo into making serious blunders that cause it to lose the game.[5]

Yet other weaknesses have been detected. In 2022, Ryuichiro Hataya, Han Bao, and Hiromi Arai discovered that AI image-generation systems trained on even massive quantities of previously AI-generated images were much less varied in appearance, being more or less a variation on a theme, than when the same systems were trained on images created by human artists.⁶ Similarly, Yanzhu Guo, Guokan Shang, Michalis Vazirgiannis, and Chloé Clavel found that text-generating AI systems showed "a marked decrease in the diversity of the models' outputs through successive iterations" (i.e., that the AI generated texts started to sound much more like each other).⁷ They conclude that "incorporating model-generated content in training may lead to irreversible flaws in the resulting models."

Of course, such flaws will almost certainly be ironed out, but new, unexpected problems will emerge both in AI and in human behavior. The internet is worth contemplating in this regard. A relatively new technology, in two decades the internet has transformed drastically. It was once a technological "Wild West" in which every user could express their opinions, and early social media platforms (such as MySpace) were largely concerned with connection and self-expression. Now dominated by large corporations, political rivalry and stereotyping of the political opposition is the norm across platforms, speech is policed, and some opinions and even facts are prohibited. People have even been prosecuted and imprisoned for opinions posted online. We should expect a similar trajectory in relation to AI, with creativity, freedom, and enthusiasm slowly giving way to increasing rules, restrictions, and undesirable consequences.

We, of course, are primarily concerned with human behavior. The best creators understand the material they are working with and understand it at the most basic level; for instance, Alexander McQueen who worked in tailoring before studying at fashion college. Yet in the not-too-distant future, creators might increasingly rely on AI to create new art or new designs. If so, they will no longer understand the limits and possibilities of the materials of their art to the same degree as previous designers.

But leaving aside the creative elite, what might occur when generations rely on AI for seemingly basic tasks such as writing, both for basic communication and for academic papers? Let's think briefly about the act of writing. Writing requires us to think not only about the subject being written about but about communicating our thoughts about the subject through language, deciding what word expresses what we want to convey in the most precise way possible. As such, writing requires us to think about thinking itself. Over time, this enables the individual to detect flaws, weaknesses, and biases in their own mental activity.

It seems plausible to imagine a scenario, at some point in the future, in which we have corporations that are populated by employees who rely on AI systems to make decision and corporate AI systems that, in turn, rely on these AI-dependent employees' feedback to generate information and ideas for those decisions to be made. If we photocopy a photocopy of an image, repeating the process of photocopying the last photocopy ad infinitum, the image of each iteration will be more distorted and degraded than the last. So likewise, we should expect all sorts of distortions and vulnerabilities to emerge in such a feedback loop of human-dependent AIs with AI-dependent humans.

AI systems are currently limited and one-dimensional. They are mostly "trained" for one particular function or task. They have blind spots and biases and they treat some data and questions as simply forbidden. But the same observations can be made about the kind of employees and college graduates that AI will almost inevitably replace and the kind of people that will almost inevitably struggle professionally and personally over the coming decades. In this chapter, then, we will explore a more holistic, authentic, and creative way of thinking and living.

This will require us to develop ourselves mentally, physically, spiritually, creatively, and culturally. And it will require us to continually explore new information and lines of thought both inside and outside of our professions, to be a conduit for new ideas. It will require us to be agile, resilient, and to be adept at managing stress and thriving under pressure. And it will require us to think more creatively and to be comfortable with taking manageable risks. As such, in this chapter we will explore the counterintuitive, which can be just as decisive a factor in life, business, design, and art as it can in Go. Indeed, the counterintuitive runs through this final guide to transforming chaos, which I am calling "the six Cs." They are (1) Connection, (2) Creativity, (3) Craft, (4) Culture, (5) Character, and (6) Consciousness. Let's begin.

CONNECTION

Throughout the twenty-first century (which promises to be a fast-changing society shaped by a knowledge economy) two kinds of connection will matter most of all: (1) connections to other people and (2) the ability to connect different ideas, concepts, and disciplines. Of course, these two different types of connection are and will remain associated.

In 1973, sociologist Mark Granovetter proposed that you are more likely to get a job through "weak ties"—acquaintances with whom you share few mutual connections, such as a friend of a friend—than through family or close friends. A recent study by LinkedIn confirmed Granovetter's intuitions, observing that it is often our weakest ties, measured by the intensity of interactions, that create the most job mobility, while strong ties create the least. Of course this varies by profession and is most especially the case in the tech industry.[8]

Strong ties of close friends and family are, of course, invaluable. But strong ties tend to have access to the same information as us. In other words, your strong ties are likely to know what you know and to be connected to the same circles of people. Weak ties, on the other hand, can transmit novel information or can make introductions to new, valuable connections.

Notably, individuals who consider themselves as "high status" tend to turn to weak ties to help them find a new position while low-status individuals tend to turn to strong ties.[9] The former also tend to actively cultivate relationships with other high-status individuals, meaning decision-makers who are influential, success minded, positive, and obsessed with self-improvement. Indeed, while 75 percent of the wealthy regularly reach out to valuable contacts, only 13 percent of low-income individuals do the same.[10]

We have spoken about weak ties in relation to wealth. However, even in this context we have mentioned self-improvement. Such ties can be invaluable for introducing new ideas, information, and connections to creative individuals like artists, writers, designers, and technological innovators, as well as to thinking individuals more broadly. Indeed, the energy of a culture is dependent on the degree to which it enables intelligent people of different backgrounds to meet, exchange ideas, and form working or personal relationships; it is through such meetings that new solutions to old problems may be inspired, new ideas formulated, new artistic movements born, and so on. Continual creativity, reinvention, and retaining or gaining a competitive advantage require serendipity.

By bringing people together from different fields or specialties the potential for serendipity increases. While she was first lady, Jacqueline Kennedy invited artists, scientists, writers, and poets to events and dinners at the White House so that they would be able to mingle with statesmen, diplomats, and politicians.[11] This was not simply a desire of the first lady alone. John F. Kennedy, who was a writer himself, enjoyed interacting with historians and scholars. Indeed, an invitation to 168 prominent "creative Americans" to attend his presidential inauguration let it be known that his administration hoped to have "a productive relationship with our writers, artists, composers, philosophers, scientists, and heads of cultural institutions."[12]

There are other ways to spark creative interactions, of course. Samsung's U.S. headquarters in San Jose was purposely designed to encourage collaboration.[13] Vast outdoor areas between floors were incorporated into the design with the hope that these communal areas would result in engineers and salespeople mingling. As Scott Birnbaum, a vice president of Samsung Semiconductor recognized, "The most creative ideas aren't going to come while sitting in front of your monitor." For this reason, he noted, Samsung's headquarters was "really designed to spark not just collaboration but that innovation you see when people collide."[14] And collision, we might note, is an aspect of chaos.

Creative and otherwise inquisitive people will sometimes cross over from one discipline to another, and more importantly perhaps, it is in their new discipline that these outsiders will often make radical new breakthroughs or innovations. Or as mathematician Benoit Mandelbrot put it, "the rare scholars who are nomads-by-choice are essential to the intellectual welfare of the settled disciplines."[15] At the beginning of this book, we mentioned physicist-turned-biologist Robert M. May, who sparked a serious interest in nonlinear systems in mathematics. Mandelbrot, too, had taught engineering at Yale, physiology at the Einstein School of Medicine, and economics at Harvard, though he would be one of the first to use computers to demonstrate that complexity can be created from simple rules, as embodied in the well-known "Mandelbrot set."[16]

Even when they do not make breakthroughs in other fields, like Mandelbrot, we find that some of the most renowned creators practice arts other than the one that they are known for. After meeting Cubist painter Amédée Ozenfant, the modernist architect Le Corbusier (Charles-Édouard Jeanneret) took up painting. The surrealist painter Salvador Dali also worked on some experimental films and jewelry. Pablo Picasso worked in painting, sculpture, and ceramics. Singer-songwriter David Bowie was also a painter and actor. And Yukio Mishima—one of Japan's greatest twentieth-century authors—was also an actor, orchestra conductor, martial artist, and bodybuilder. Samuel Morse, the inventor of Morse code, studied painting at London's Royal Academy, as well as mathematics and philosophy at Yale. And the father of modern neuroscience, Santiago Ramón y Cajal, also originally wanted to become an artist. As a scientist, he used his artistic skills to draw, using pen and ink, the cell structure of brains.[17]

It is not unusual for artistic people from different disciplines to form circles of friends. Often what is valuable in these relationships is not the potential to make financially lucrative connections but rather the transmission of ideas and novel information from disciplines that an individual creator has little connection to or understanding of. Sometimes a creator from one discipline can connect to a field that, superficially at least, seems entirely unrelated. In 2015, artist Antoni De Lenval Malinowski was commissioned to paint a mural on two large walls of the foyer of Oxford University's Mathematical Institute. Like Malinowski's previous work, the mural was painstakingly composed of tens of thousands of tiny brush strokes. To Malinowski's surprise, at the private view of the mural, some of the university's mathematicians described the work as a "stochastic masterpiece." Stochastic mathematics deals with the discovery of patterns in seeming randomness or chaos. Malinowski had never thought of his work as related to mathematics.[18]

With new information stimulating new ideas or possibilities for creative expression in the recipients, groups of creatives from different fields, even if meeting infrequently, can be especially useful to avoid intellectual or artistic stagnation. We can think of such groups of creatives as hubs of informational weak ties. If, for example, a painter is introduced to a specific aspect of an author's work that has some intellectual resonance with his own, he does not need to study the entirety of the author's oeuvre, or literature more generally, but can hone in on this one aspect. Nevertheless, we do find creators who will explore in-depth the works of creatives in other fields; for example, the British artist David Hockney painted several works that were influenced by the American poet Walt Whitman. We also find collaborations between creators in different fields. Notably, in 1937 Salvador Dali worked with fashion designer Elsa Schiaparelli for her collection that year, and more recently, Japanese artist Yoshitomo Nara collaborated with fashion designer Stella McCartney.

Particularly in a fast-changing world such as ours, wide connectivity is essential for professional prospects and for problem-solving, creativity, and intellectual and even spiritual vibrancy. This does not mean jumping from one field to another or misusing other people's generosity. Genuine relationships need to be cultivated and this requires giving, not just taking. In regard to the absorption of ideas, this means thinking deeply about new information and allowing ourselves to be adaptable. Yet it also means refining the raw information, integrating it deeply into our own processes, and creating something new.

CREATIVITY

When it comes to success in the life of the individual and the success of the nation as a whole, in the West we tend to believe that IQ is the most important factor. Institutionally, over the last few decades, English-speaking countries have tended to look down upon the arts. Popularly viewed as little more than a break from real learning, when the education budget shrinks, art classes tend to be cut first or most.[19] However, the correlation between lifetime creative achievement—such as becoming an inventor, software developer, entrepreneur, author, diplomat, doctor, or college president—and high childhood CQ (creative quotient, or creative ability) is three times stronger than with high childhood IQ. To put it more plainly, a high level of creativity in childhood is three times more likely to result in a highly successful life in adulthood than high intelligence during the same period.[20]

During the twenty-first century, creative ability will be increasingly important in business. To think differently and to be able to do more with less will give companies and individuals an edge. Yet CQ in America has been in decline since around 1990. In 2010, Jonathan Plucker of Indiana University visited schools in Beijing and Shanghai. There he saw that students were encouraged to think outside the box. He was amazed to see that, for a science project, one high school student had configured a tracking device from his moped to parts of his cellphone. Faculty at one Chinese university asked Plucker about trends in American education. When he told them it was standardized testing and rote memorization they laughed and told him that while the Chinese were adopting the United States' old, successful model of education, America was rushing to adopt the old—and failed—Chinese model.[21]

Computer scientist Alan Kay once remarked, "a change in perspective is worth 80 IQ points."[22] At the foundational level, creativity requires us to change the way we think about something. In 1967, British psychologist Liam Hudson (1933–2005) published his paper "Contrary Imaginations: A Psychological Study of the English Schoolboy." In it, he introduced the divergence test. In contrast to the IQ test (or "convergence" tests generally) the point of Hudson's test is not to reduce the number of possibilities for each question and to "converge" on the correct answer. Rather, it was to find as many different solutions to a proposed problem as possible.

Hudson asked students to write down as many things as possible that you could do with a brick and a blanket. There are probably an almost unlimited number of things you could do with either. You could use a brick in building a house, but you could easily use it as a doorstop, paperweight, hammer, coaster for a couple of hot drinks, or an ultramodern incense burner (assuming it is one of those bricks with the indentation). Surprisingly however, Hudson discovered that those with high IQ often scored poorly on his divergence test, giving no more examples than would be obvious to anyone. They lacked imagination. Or to put it another way, they lacked the ability to look at things differently and to see the possibilities.

Inventiveness requires knowledge—preferably of different fields. But looking at things differently, rather than "correctly," is a crucial part of how we get new inventions, discoveries, scientific breakthroughs, and solutions to new problems. It is also essential to research, fiction writing, and to copywriting and marketing. Indeed, in discussing the features and benefits of products, copywriter Robert Bly gives the example of a pencil and lists more than ten benefits, among them "writes smoothly yet crisply," "easy to hold and comfortable to write with," and "long writing life."[23] We can even add a few more: a pencil is lightweight, easily transportable, can be used to write on multiple surfaces, and—in a time when we are used to being sent impersonal messages and images over the web—we can use a pencil to write or draw a little something that the recipient will be able to keep and perhaps display on their apartment or office wall. We might even say that the pencil is the tool of an artist.

Most people think of a pencil as "just a pencil" and a brick as "just a brick." And this attitude seeps into every aspect of life, personal and professional. Everything is done according to how it was always done, until it grinds to a halt or—more likely in the twenty-first century—until it is replaced by some sort of artificial intelligence.

Divergent thinking often means seeing how different and even entirely unrelated things can be brought together. Inspired by calligraphy classes that he had taken at Reed College, Steve Jobs introduced fonts to computing. Fashion designer Issey Miyake drew on origami, the traditional Japanese art of paper folding, to construct clothing in new ways. The French impressionist painters Mary Cassatt, Edgar Degas, and Claude Monet were influenced by Japanese woodblock prints. Hip-hop musicians have often incorporated other genres of music—including classical music—into their compositions, even though their fans might have hated the genre or song that they sampled. To create something new and unexpected, we often have to look back to the past or to a different discipline.

Making mistakes can also be important to creativity. In any creative process, a mistake produces something different. Most of the time such mistakes may not be valuable. But some are. In 1968, Spencer F. Silver invented the adhesive that would later be used for Post-It Notes. Silver mentioned his invention to his colleagues at 3M, the company where he was working, and over several years he attempted to make the glue stronger. Over half a decade had passed when in 1974, a chemical engineer by the name of Art Fry was at church one morning and was growing frustrated that his bookmarks kept falling out of his hymnal. Thinking that it would be useful if there were bookmarks that could be stuck in the hymnal—but that could be peeled off without damaging it—Fry recalled Silver's adhesive. The not-so-sticky glue had found its purpose.[24]

If Silver had been thinking divergently rather than convergently he would have realized that there are lots of things you could do with a not-so-sticky adhesive. From the humble bookmark, some people are now creating works of art out of Post-It Notes, placing them side-by-side to create giant, pixel-like images of everything from computer game characters to Marilyn Monroe. Whoever first thought of making art out of these somewhat sticky squares of paper was thinking divergently. The artist almost certainly had a lower IQ than Silver but perhaps they possessed greater CQ. Certainly they possessed greater perceptual curiosity.

Making mistakes is part of the process of making art, regardless of whether the art in question is painting, fashion, or music. Sometimes the artist has an idea that doesn't work out and then changes direction. But occasionally, the artist keeps the mistake because it is better than what was intended.

After The Beatles and Wings, Paul McCartney found that his music had lost its edge. To make matters worse, he was surrounded by people who were too agreeable to challenge him. Recognizing the problem, McCartney decided to work with Nigel Godrich, who was known for producing much darker and edgier musicians. In the process of recording McCartney's album *Chaos and Creation in the Backyard*, the former Beatles star was playing his song "Fine Line" on the piano. At one point, McCartney hit the wrong note. It was a mistake. But Goodrich made McCartney keep it in the final recording, saying later that it was his "favorite moment in the song," and that it just made you "perk up your ears" and listen to it.[25]

Creativity is often described in such terms as *curiosity, open-mindedness, flexibility, counterintuitive thinking, contrarianism, innovation*, and *novelty*. But creativity requires a degree of daring. To create or invent something new is to risk being ridiculed. Creativity requires looking at things differently and envisioning possibilities that other people do not—and that, in many cases, will be opposed by a large number of people who are attached to the status quo. Take, for example, the French Impressionists. We tend to view their work as rather innocent. Yet the movement scandalized France during its day, partly because of the innovative style of painting and partly because some of the paintings were of prostitutes.

There are times when creative ideas don't work well in practice. During World War I, British and American ships were sometimes disguised with a style of camouflage named Razzle Dazzle. This was composed of very large, very thick, angular, black-and-white lines that visually distorted the shape of the ship and theoretically made it difficult to see which way it was sailing. The flaw in the plan, of course, was that it made ships easy to spot in the first place. Highly creative, Razzle Dazzle was eventually abandoned for more sensible camouflage, mostly solid gray.

Art is different from creativity. An individual who paints in the style of the nineteenth-century French Impressionists today may be highly artistic but not necessarily very creative. Copying a historical style might suggest that the individual is uncreative and perhaps even rather conservative in their taste. AI is already able to mimic such art. Indeed, it can already create photographic-like images and footage of (generated) people. It seems likely that in most cases, skill will not be enough to prevent an artist's work from being devalued by AI. Skill might even seem antiquated. In probably almost every profession, instead of relying on the mere repetition of a formula, we will need to be agile, adaptable, and able to think differently. In contrast, an inventor who makes some new technological breakthrough or the CEO who is able to see and exploit a gap in the market might be highly creative even if they are not in the slightest bit artistic.

Nevertheless, the arts and creativity coincide to a very significant degree, largely because art schools tend to want to push students to be experimental and to push the boundaries of their chosen field. But all art colleges and courses are not equal. Some are culturally insignificant while others have produced many of the world's best-known artists and designers. Fashion graduates of the London-based Central Saint Martins College of Art and Design (C.S.M.) include Alexander McQueen, John Galliano, Hussein Chalayan, Stella McCartney, Katharine Hamnett, Sarah Burton (who designed Kate Middleton's royal wedding dress), Zac Posen, Mary Katrantzou, Phoebe Philo (a former creative director of both Chloé and Céline who now has her own label), and Riccardo Tisci (a creative director of Givenchy and Burberry).*

"Fashion is everywhere," bestselling author and founder of direct marketing company Yoyodyne, Seth Godin, has said.[26] By fashion, however, he means not just clothing but music, the food we eat, the political policies that get enacted, and ultimately, the way we look at the world. Change is constant but few industries outside of fashion recognize this and even fewer are in a state of perpetual reinvention and transformation; fashion designers create something new each season, several times a year.

In his book *What They Don't Teach You at Harvard Business School*, Mark H. McCormack laments that a business education can foster serious limits in the thinking of graduates, leading to an inability to understand, or wrongly interpreting, business situations or people. "Obviously, neither people nor problems fit molds," he says, "and the very act of trying to make them do so distorts perceptions."[27] This leads to bad decisions in both business and life. But business education's attempt to get students to think within the box is the exact opposite of what C.S.M. attempts to do.

In a 2011 article pondering why the college was so successful, the BBC observed that of the 86 designers showing at London Fashion Week, almost half (41) were C.S.M. graduates. Notably, well over 300 fashion design courses are offered by colleges in the United Kingdom.[28] Let's look at some of the characteristics of studying at C.S.M.:

1. Exposure to ideas: Students are introduced to art and design movements both old and new, well-known and more obscure: the latest fashion design, fine artists, photographers, and filmmakers, as well as historical movements from baroque to punk. They are also introduced to British, European, and global culture.

---

*Although she went into fashion design and modeling only briefly after graduating, the Nigerian-born singer Sade is also a fashion graduate of C.S.M.

2. Creative environment: As *i-D* magazine has noted, fashion students at Central Saint Martins are taught by both full-time teachers and by famous contemporary designers, or "part-time and visiting tutors from fashion's Hall of Fame."[29] But crucially, there are also influences from outside of fashion. "I had a lot of interaction with people from the fine art and sculpture departments, which really affected my outlook," said fashion designer Hussein Chalayan, reflecting on his time as a student at the college.[30] Such interactions are common at Saint Martins, and fine art students at the college have a reputation for being intellectual and experimental. Moreover, for most of its life, Saint Martins was located on the edge of Soho in central London (it relocated to Kings Cross in 2012), close to museums, art galleries, fashion designer boutiques, and book shops, as well as the kinds of nightclubs, bars, and cafes that attract the more avant-garde type of individual.

3. Encouragement to think differently: *The Daily Telegraph*'s fashion correspondent Hilary Alexander, has described the training at the college as rigorous in regard to skill but "very anti-establishment" in regard to ideas.[31] And Giles Deacon (British Designer of the Year, 2006) said of Louise Wilson (1962–2014), the college's most formidable M.A. fashion professor, "She teaches you how to think for yourself."[32] Translation: exploring unusual ideas, thoughts, and elements of culture to see whether this will contribute to a creative or aesthetic breakthrough.

4. Encouragement to ask questions: To create something that is novel and valuable, a creator has to ask the right questions. This requires the individual to understand the material they are working with and the standard methods and their limits, and to ponder how these might be changed. In regard to fashion, one might wonder, *What will happen if I mix these two different things together?* (such as Punk and Victorian dress); *What*

happens if I use a material for clothing that is intended for something else? (Chalayan had made clothing out of paper in his final year at CSM); *How do I subvert expectations so that I can surprise and excite?* And so on. At C.S.M., playing it safe, copying, and mainstream interests and taste are considered decidedly déclassé.

5. Encouragement to make novel connections: We have already spoken about connection, of course. Exposure to interesting people, new ideas, and artistic and design movements is only step one. At some point, the student must focus on some of these influences and integrate them into their work to create something unexpected. Notably, throughout his career, McQueen drew inspiration from a vast array of sources, including the designs of William Morris, the fairy tales of the Brothers Grimm, and Martin Scorsese's movie *Taxi Driver*.[33]

6. Cultivation of daring and resilience: From the outside, the world of high fashion looks extremely glamorous. And it is. But it is also incredibly demanding and cutthroat. A designer can be catapulted to fame when they are new and unprepared for the limelight and then trashed by the press the next season. Encouragement to be yourself and to explore unique areas of interest comes as a package deal with very harsh criticism of completed projects. "They say if you can survive Louise, you can survive the industry," is how one M.A. fashion student put it.[34] The same goes for B.A. lessons. C.S.M. students have to take on board the message that they can do much better and then get on with the next project, push themselves harder, and face the possibility of more harsh criticism, usually in front of every other student in the class.

CRAFT

I happened to be in Alexander McQueen's studio one evening during his early days as a designer. He was already famous but wasn't living—

or dressing—like it. The studio was a cramped space in a basement in Belgravia. He had to make a dress for his backer Isabella Blow, who was going to wear it to an event the following evening. McQueen told me he had put off making it ("for months," if I recall correctly). Then, in front of me, he laid out some fabric, took a yardstick, and drew out the shape of a dress (with sleeves). Then he told his assistant to cut it out and sew it up, and left ("going to the pub"). I thought he was mad. He came from a working-class background and seemed like it; then, everyone knew McQueen by his first name, Lee. Blow could—and later did—make McQueen a star. Despite his extraordinary skill, in the cut-throat world of high fashion, without her, he might have been sunk. The next time I saw him, he told me, grinning, "she loved it."

Before attending Central Saint Martins, McQueen had worked for Savile Row tailors. He knew his craft inside and out. This is something that he shared with the greatest inventors, artists, and designers of history, from Leonardo da Vinci to Pablo Picasso. Such innovators have always combined divergent thinking with an extremely high level of skill and humble dedication to their craft—not uncommonly supplemented with a little public arrogance and showmanship.

Yet today, it is common for managers with no practical skills to make decisions over processes that they have no direct experience of, including in the different design fields. Indeed, bad management is common in every field of business,[35] costing U.S. companies far in excess of a trillion dollars a year in loss of productivity and employee turnover.[36]

During its early days, Apple hired a number of professional managers from outside the company. But Steve Jobs soon fired them. "They knew how to manage," he would later recall, "but they didn't know how to do anything." After that, Jobs paid no attention to resumes or prior experience in his search for a manager for the brand. Instead, he wanted someone who was passionate about technology and knew where it was headed. He also "wanted people that were insanely great at what they did." Jobs hired Debi Coleman, a thirty-two-year-old English literature graduate. She was already an employee of Apple and she met the criteria that Jobs was looking for. Three years later, she had risen to become Apple's CFO.[37]

Though essential, skill is not enough by itself. As Dean Keith Simonton has observed, "increased expertise can often bring about decreased creativity." He cites the example of the Italian opera composer Pietro Macagni, "whose best opera was his first,"[38] with a gradual but steady decline thereafter. His creativity deteriorating with each work, eventually his audiences began booing him. But let's be honest: we can all think of authors and aging pop stars whose work becomes less and less daring, more and more vanilla, and each new book or song more and more a bad copy of their previous work. Skill must be married to creativity.

While many elements of human culture can be reproduced cheaply and easily, with little human thought or expertise anywhere involved in the process, if it can be combined with creativity, mastery of a skill often demands our attention and money. We can order a burger for a few dollars at a fast-food restaurant in probably every part of the world. And they all taste pretty much the same. At De Daltons diner in Voorthuizen, Netherlands, their "Golden Boy" burger is made with A5 Japanese Wagyu beef, chuck short ribs, white truffles, Paleta Iberico Bellota ham, and Beluga caviar. Other ingredients include Dom Perignon champagne, Kopi Luwak coffee, and Macallan single malt whiskey. Price tag: $6,000.[39]

Similarly, though they may serve a purpose, easily accessible stock art and generic music are cheap and unexciting. In contrast, we will often go out of our way to see fine art in a gallery or to listen to live music, and in many cases, we expect the price tag to be high. Quality is one reason why we will seek out an original painting in a gallery or a live music experience. Rarity is another. AI will make some aspects of culture, such as digital imagery, more accessible, but with easy access and instantaneity, mass production will also make these same aspects of culture boring and cheap.

Craft connects us to rarity, authenticity, and character. None of us marvel at the speed of a car or an airplane but, even though they are much slower in comparison, we become excited, even fixated, watching a race between athletes or even between horses. Of course, there is motor racing, but at the end of the race we watch the winning driver receiving a trophy and splashing champagne everywhere. It is the human element—the character of the driver—that ultimately matters. Character implies a history of overcoming personal struggles and obstacles. We can find it in athletics just as we can find it in art or fashion.

Unsurprisingly, in recent years we have seen a renewed interest in traditional skills such as organic farming, craft beer, and upcycled clothing. In Italy, where youth unemployment has been at nearly 40 percent, the country has been reviving its traditional crafts, such as tailoring and shoemaking, and having young people take on apprenticeships. It has helped to boost the economy and has led to Italians "rediscovering their entrepreneurial spirit" and launching small artisanal businesses, including in traditional pasta-making.[40] The renewed focus on craft is also helping to sustain the image of "made in Italy" as one of premium quality.

Luxury brands outside of Italy are also investing in traditional crafts. In 2023, Parisian fashion house Dior turned to traditional Indian textile crafts, working with artisans at the Chanakya atelier for its fall collection, shown in Mumbai.[41] The techniques used included hand embroidery and *shisheh* (small mirrors attached to cloth with embroidery) and other techniques dating back to the Mughal era or earlier. Known for its fashion and accessories, Hermès revived the town of Montbron in France after it discovered its traditional and artisanal leather workshop. The workshop had closed and the town was economically depressed, but after discovering it, the luxury fashion brand invested in the town and reopened the facility, creating 250 new jobs and reviving what might have become a lost art.[42]

Here we might pause to reflect on the age-old saying, "you have to change with the times." But this isn't entirely true, is it? In reality, there are three responses to changing times: (1) keep doing what you are doing until your work is made obsolete, (2) change with the times, or (3) change against the times. Or, do a combination of the aforementioned. The leather workshop of Montbron lost business and eventually closed because it kept doing what it was doing even though it was unable to compete in a changing world of mass production. It was later revived by Hermès, who was acting *against* the times, bringing back artistry. In an era of mass-produced, cheaply made products intended to be obsolete or fall apart after a few years at most, artistry is rarity, authenticity (meaning history, cultural tradition, and the handmade), and character. And, of course, it demands a premium price. At the same time, however, Hermès uses the latest technology in other areas, especially in customer experience. Notably, the brand is already looking to establish itself in the metaverse or Web3.[43]

Undoubtedly, it is possible to approach modern technology as a craft. However, over the next few decades an increasingly large percentage of the population of industrialized nations will believe that they do not need to acquire general, cultural, or historical knowledge. They will realize that artificial intelligence can provide them with almost instant access to facts and that it will eliminate any need to be able to compose any kind of communication sent electronically. AI can probably already produce written and visual material that is more than "good enough" for the average person to consume and even to stimulate them emotionally. And of course, when a large language model or some other type of future technology produces an opinion that they like, the average citizen will proclaim it to be the authority that we should trust.

Yet this will be detrimental both to the individual and to society. Let's think about this via analogy: Americans walk less than people in any other industrialized nation, or probably the world. "We've engineered walking out of our existence and everyday life," notes Tom Vanderbilt. And he is correct. People will drive to places they could easily walk to. But as Americans have decreased their time walking certain health problems (such as obesity*) have increased.[44] Human beings were designed to walk.

Although it is sometimes difficult to believe, human beings were also designed to think and to find creative solutions to problems. Hundreds of thousands of years ago, it was our ability to think, to imagine, to plan, and to cooperate that enabled us to avoid being killed by predators, and to hunt animals much larger and more ferocious than us—and thus to survive. Perhaps we will see a rise in serious mental health problems such as depression and dementia as a result of relying on technology to think for us. But certainly those who use technology as a kind of substitute brain will see their own intelligence and creative ability atrophy and will be unable to properly evaluate whatever the technology produces. They will have data and information at their fingertips but will not understand its full implications. They will lack wisdom.

Of course, the consumer-minded majority may not demand either logical argument or an elite level in design. But those who wish to thrive in the future will be society's most thoughtful and creative. The only way to do this is to develop skills, study different intellectual fields, and develop an appreciation for material culture and culture creators. We have mentioned McQueen. Part of what made him so incredible as a designer was his experience working from the bottom up. He knew every technical detail of how to create a garment but he wasn't limited by his technical skill. He was limited only by his imagination.

We also mentioned Jobs firing the outside managers that Apple had hired. Whatever may have been the case there, leaders who don't understand what their subordinates do or how they do it are usually less capable of leading and being effective. A manager with such a serious knowledge gap might even begin to view their most talented

---

*Like all health conditions, obesity is complex and may have several different causes. However, a nutritious diet and daily exercise, such as walking, are the rock-bottom requirements to maintain health.

subordinates as a threat, and this will mean that the manager will try to stay on top by manipulating, rather than supporting, their team.

By removing any need to do low-level tasks, AI will create serious gaps in the knowledge and experience of leaders, making them less able to make decisions or even to act on intuition. In what might become a vicious cycle, this in turn will make them more dependent on AI. Undoubtedly we will eventually see even some large corporations fail as a result.

It is probable that in the coming decades, developing our intelligence and creativity will not only be seen as essential for CEOs and entrepreneurs but will (along with fitness and routine meditation-type exercises) be regarded as integral to wellness and personal growth. Despite AI's ability to do it for us, developing creativity will require individuals to develop different, premodern, and even rather basic skills: painting, writing, music, martial arts, and dance, as well as philosophy, logic, and so on. We will explore this momentarily in the section on Character.

CULTURE

We tend to think of culture as cuisine, fine art, classical music, and couture clothing or tailored suits. But culture (from the Latin word *cultura*, meaning "cultivate" or "agriculture") is really what is cultivated by a group, usually over a long period of time. This includes food, aesthetics like art and clothing, and music, yes. But it also includes such intangible things as philosophy, religion or lack thereof, law, assumptions about life, group identity, group rituals, humor, and so on.

At the most fundamental level then, culture is the narrative that society tells itself. And to a very significant degree, everything else (the arts, the sciences, etc.) emerges through that narrative. Hence, as we have seen, in Europe, where the notion of the individual as opposed to the tribe or family was seemingly first developed, giving birth to psychology and the self-help industry much later on, the portrait was regarded as the pinnacle of fine art painting, whereas in China, where the collective was more important, the landscape assumed this place. And under Islam, where devotion to God was more important, geometric patterns became the essential element of the visual arts, especially where artists were prohibited from portraying human beings or elements of nature.

Narratives can change the way we see things and the way we feel. From Pericles to Napoleon Bonaparte, great generals have been great speakers. Through their words, spoken with conviction and feeling, they have been able to dispel the fears and despondency of their troops. And they have been able to instill the belief that they are great men carrying out a historic mission and, importantly, that they will win (or in the worst-case scenario, that they will attain glory through death). This has often made the difference between victory and defeat.

Of course the same is often true for leaders in other fields, including professors, CEOs, and—at least in the past—national leaders. Hence Franklin D. Roosevelt's inaugural address to the American people in 1933, when he uttered the still oft-repeated phrase "the only thing we have to fear is fear itself." At the time, the United States was in an economic depression with mass unemployment. People were afraid for their future. Roosevelt recast the very notion of fear, effectively telling the nation that the only thing that stood in the way of an economic recovery was this emotion or, to put it another way, the irrational.

Storytelling can strengthen bonds and increase cooperation. A team of researchers led by anthropologists Daniel Smith, Andrea Migliano, and Lucio Vinicius of the anthropology department of University College London began studying two communities of the Indigenous hunter-gatherer Agta tribe in the Philippines' Isabela Province. Each of the communities was made up of multiple camps.

In the first study, the researchers asked 297 people spread across the two communities to vote for the best storytellers. Then they gave 290 different people in the communities twelve tokens each. These could be exchanged for a small amount of rice. The participants were told that they could keep their tokens or give any or all of them away. Unsurprisingly, on average, participants kept just over 60 percent of the tokens for themselves. However, as the remainder of the tokens were distributed among the Agta, a pattern emerged. Camps with a greater proportion of respected storytellers received more tokens (2.2 percent more rice for every 1 percent more storyteller).

Next, the researchers asked 291 members of the communities to name up to five people they would be happy to live with. Skilled storytellers were almost twice as likely to be picked as the other community members who were named and favored, even over those with a good reputation for hunting, fishing, and foraging for food. It may be that humans simply enjoy hearing stories, but those told by the Agta not only humanized nature (e.g., animals and planets), they also championed social norms and group cooperation.[45] In other words, they gave meaning and purpose to the Agta people themselves.

In modern societies, narratives can create meaning and change our perception. A fake Jackson Pollock painting is nothing more than drips on canvas. We won't knowingly go out of our way to view it, though we will go to a museum or gallery to spend time looking at an original (or a forgery that we think is an original), even though there may be no difference in quality between the fake and the real thing. It is impossible to know how many paintings in major museums are fakes but Britain's *Independent* newspaper has estimated that it is probably around 20 percent.[46] If this is correct almost every museum-goer and art lover has marveled at a fake, thinking it to be authenic.

So why do we pay attention to the work of an artist but prefer to ignore fakes of equal quality in the same style? It is the story about the painting, sculpture, or other artifact that fascinates us. An authentic work of art connects us to a moment in time: the sixties, the Roaring Twenties, the Renaissance, and so on. And it connects us to the human genius that saw how something unique could be created in that moment, challenging convention and enabling us to see things differently—to see new possibilities. So, a period of time has its story; an artist has a story, which usually involves overcoming some sort of hardship or personal challenges; and thus, an authentic work of art has its story too.

But what is true of our relationship to the arts is also true of our relationship to things in general, including wine, chocolate, and even painkillers. When wine has a higher price, the reward centers of our brain light up and we experience it as tasting better than the same wine priced more cheaply.[47] Cheap wine is just something to swill down half-heartedly. With expensive wine, we imagine sunny French vineyards and a more idyllic lifestyle. It is a story. Similarly, as marketing genius Rory Sutherland has observed, branded painkillers are more effective than generic ones—when they have the exact same ingredients.[48]

In complex societies, there are different, competing, and even contradictory narratives about what the culture of a nation represents and what it should represent. In China, despite conflicts between them early on, Buddhism, Taoism, and Confucianism came to be viewed as the "three teachings" that illuminated the individual's duty toward the self, nature, and society respectively. In other cases—often without any sense of dissonance—a nation may have a pacifist religion but also a powerful military. Within the nation-state, social, political, and other types of voluntary societies attract people when they (1) have a prestigious history, (2) are able to exert significant influence in society or in a particular field in the present time, or (3) have a compelling vision for the future. Or, as in religious cults, an organization might attract people through promises of secret wisdom, spiritual enlightenment, or freedom from particular internal struggles, such as drug addiction or depression.

If the nation is unified by an overarching worldview or by a belief in its greatness—especially if groups and individuals holding different views are relatively weak or lack significant support—then these smaller groups can be held together in relative harmony, despite their differences. But if the unifying belief begins to weaken, perhaps because of substantial economic decline, or comes to be regarded as morally wrong, tension will increase significantly within society and the gaps between the movements or cultures within it can widen to the point where hostility turns into open conflict.

Even large groups, organizations, and corporations can be affected for similar reasons. Instead of putting the corporation first, a manager might vie for power with other managers and might even try to dispose of any subordinates competent enough to pose a threat to their prestige. This will, of course, undermine productivity, creativity, and problem-solving. If left unchecked, it will eventually negatively affect the company, perhaps even leading to serious financial loss or collapse.

Fragmentation can also lead to the collapse of a nation or, being perceived as weak, unpredictable, and with less wealth, can contribute to the weakening of its effectiveness on the world stage. At the same time, it is possible that such fragmentation will facilitate the articulation of new ideas, the creation of artistic and literary styles, new fashions, new religious cults, new lifestyles, and so on. Nevertheless, relatively short-lived periods of anarchic creativity tend to be followed by longer periods of authoritarianism. We see this in politics and we see this in culture more generally.

Societies that are able to navigate challenging periods and survive or grow have (1) a strong sense of mission, (2) relatively strong bonds and loyalty to the group and to one another, (3) leaders and groups who are able to anticipate and adapt to changing circumstances and who do not need to wait for instructions from above, and (4) members with different skills, interests, specialist knowledge, and life experiences who can illuminate different areas of potential risk and reward.

Let's look at business. It has become the norm for U.S. corporations to expect their employees to work long hours. And even when it is not explicitly required, employees will often feel that they have to be seen showing dedication and putting in extra hours, even if that means dragging out tasks or wasting time. While burnout may also be to blame, as work hours increase, after a certain point productivity decreases. A study by Stanford University has found that a seventy-hour work week is "little different" from a fifty-six-hour work week in terms of productivity.[49] However, there can be no disputing the fact that many successful entrepreneurs work far more than average.

So why do long hours work sometimes and not others? Firstly, an entrepreneur can choose at any point to stop working on their business. Employees don't usually have that control. Employees usually have to please their immediate boss, while not doing so well as to appear to be a potential rival, whereas entrepreneurs and CEOs do not have such concerns. And of course, entrepreneurs, CEOs, and others at company decision-making levels are also often engaged in problem-solving and other mentally challenging and inspiring work, whereas employees may be doing more menial tasks and will rarely engage in imaginative, big-picture thinking.

Unsurprisingly then, it has been found that engaging in a creative hobby outside of work correlates with increased creativity and a better attitude at work.[50] We have spoken about the importance of bringing different ideas from different fields together. And we have noted that breakthroughs in a field are often made by those who come from a different field. An organization of people, all pursuing different creative fields in their own time, is an organization that has the potential to bring lots of unique insights and ideas together.

Nevertheless, like everyone else, business leaders can benefit from pursuing some interests or activities outside of work. Generally referred to as leisure interests or hobbies, mentally stimulating and sometimes physically challenging, these interests should be—and nearly always are—significantly more than a pleasing distraction.

Every creative person knows that solutions come in moments of inspiration when they relax. Sometimes they might have switched to doing or working on something else. Occasionally they might even be dreaming, meditating, in self-hypnosis, or just going for a walk. The ancient Greek inventor Archimedes realized how he could measure the volume of an irregular object when he stepped into a bath. We have also noted Mandelbrot's background in engineering, physiology, and economics, as well as his breakthrough in modeling complexity. And we have seen that McQueen drew on a wide range of unlikely sources—from fairy tales to movies—for his work in fashion design.

Archimedes, Mandelbrot, McQueen, and other creative thinkers associate seemingly unrelated things, sometimes (as in the case of Archimedes) solving a particular problem and sometimes (as in the case of McQueen) creating new design aesthetics. As *Harvard Business Review* has said, this ability is "central" to innovation.[51] We will look at creativity again very soon but, for now, let's think about character.

CHARACTER

We have already explored character, especially through the eight laws of self-empowerment (physical presence, self-confidence, determination, will power, fearlessness, concentration of thought, self-possession, and perception). To this, we could add such characteristics as being true to one's word or being aware of the feelings of others. All of this would be useful. But here we want to explore the idea of the whole human being through, especially, classical models. However, we want to develop ourselves as whole people partly to make connections between the different areas of our lives and thereby increase our creative potential.

The ancient Greek philosopher Aristotle claimed that there were five virtues of thought: science (*episteme*); craft, art, or skill (*techne*); practical wisdom or "prudence" (*phronesis*); understanding that enables rational thought (*nous*); and wisdom (*sophia*).[52] As the development of sophisticated technology shows, human beings are or have the capacity to be highly intelligent. Often, though, highly intelligent human beings lack wisdom or even common sense.

If we regard AI as an intelligence rather than as merely a tool, we might agree that it is or will be more intelligent than any single human being alive. But detached from nature and the physical body in meaningful ways, it will also likely be even more unwise and likely to formulate "solutions" to problems that create even more significant—although perhaps different—problems. The intellect is *ratio*. It is the brain without a body, spirit, emotions, a sense of the transcendent, and so on. It is a brain that thinks it can figure reality out in the abstract. Human beings have tried this and it has nearly always led to disaster.

A return to wisdom will be synonymous with character. And we will develop wisdom and character when we develop ourselves as a whole, broadly in line with the ancient Greek philosopher Plato's notion of education of the intellect, the training of the body, and the cultivation of the emotions, intuition, a sense of proportion and harmony, and so on. For Plato, these had to be cultivated through the practice of philosophy, wrestling, and music respectively. Unsurprisingly, we can find parallel systems of education and personal development elsewhere. China's classical Six Arts (*Liu Yi*) were ritual, music, language, arithmetic, archery, and charioteering. In Japan, there is the notion of *bunbu-ryodo* or the practice of both the martial arts and literature; we often find that the practice of, for example, *Kendo* (fencing) and poetry go hand-in-hand with the practice of Zen meditation.

In most cases, during this century the more intelligent decision-making members of society will use AI as part of their daily work, but outside of work they will spend less time on the internet and with AI than the least intelligent members of society. In effect, tomorrow's creative leaders will balance the *ratio* of work with *intellectus*, the latter of which will require switching off from technology periodically—both outside and inside of work hours. But at the highest levels of business and development, this switching off will facilitate more than clearing the mind of useless chatter. It will facilitate inspiration and the discovery of nonlogical solutions to challenges.

At the upper echelons of society, forming connections in the physical world will create greater trust and will become a marker of prestige and social proof, especially where travel is involved. Such connections will be especially necessary since filters will alter (and improve) an individual's appearance and, moreover, audio and visual fakes of individuals will be produced, sometimes with the intention of extracting personal or professional secrets or of sabotaging the reputation of an individual or corporation.

Ultimately the more successful and intelligent members of society will meet offline to get a "sense" of the people they are connected to and want to work with. Only offline will we be able to observe reactions, facial expressions, manners, posture, and how people interact with other people. And only offline will we be able to form bonds through the exchange of small gestures. As such, physical health, fitness, and personal style will be essential to forming the correct impression, especially as health declines among the least successful segments of society due in part to an overreliance on technology. Character and the ability to provide wise counsel, professionally and personally, will solidify relationships. We have already touched on some aspects but let's look briefly again at the physical, mental, and spiritual aspects of life.

1. Physical

We spoke about physical training earlier on and we mentioned martial arts. Notably, Joris Merks-Benjaminsen (head of research at Google Benelux) is a black belt in Aikido and Judo and a Brazilian Jiu-Jitsu European Champion and Open German Champion. Jeannette Wing (V.P. of Microsoft Research International) is a 4th-degree black belt in the Korean martial art of Tang Soo Do.[53] And Dan Schulman (CEO of PayPal Holdings Inc.) practices the Israeli martial art of Krav Maga every morning and believes it helps develop the leadership skills that he uses in business.[54] He is undoubtedly correct.

In a study of nearly a hundred M.B.A. students and their supervisors, James Burton (a professor in the Management Department in the NIU College of Business) found that individuals are more likely to feel belittled or abused when their supervisors are under stress. However, supervisors who engaged in regular physical exercise were less abusive.[55] CEOs who are also marathon runners have also been found to be 5 percent more effective than their less physically fit competitors.[56]

2. Mental

A number of high-profile business leaders studied philosophy at university. These include Peter Thiel (cofounder of PayPal), Gerald Levin (former Time Warner CEO), and Stewart Butterfield (cofounder of Flickr).[57]

Earlier, we discussed ratio (rational thought) and intellectus (contemplation). And we have looked at the use of rhetoric and "magic words" to manipulate and motivate people. Nevertheless, as we have said, in our fast-changing world in which little seems permanent or long-lasting, we tend to conflate intelligence with rational thinking. But while we need to adapt and to make decisions as circumstances change, we also need to cultivate long-term thinking or contemplation. It often takes years to understand ourselves and to understand any subject to the point where we can be successfully innovative. Moreover, innovation, creativity, and genius all require the work of the subconscious—gestating an idea and seeing how it connects to other information.

3. *Spiritual*

Spirituality might superficially seem to have little or nothing to do with success, especially in business. Perhaps you even think of spirituality as the polar opposite of business. But in a certain sense, spirituality returns us to connection—especially to an awareness of who we are at a deep level and to meaning and purpose in our lives, which ultimately must be expressed through what we do. In *Sacred Hoops*, Phil Jackson has said that,

> the most effective way to forge a winning team is to call on the players' need to connect with something larger than themselves. Even for those who don't consider themselves "spiritual" in a conventional sense, creating a successful team—whether it's an NBA champion or a record-setting sales force—is essentially a spiritual act.[58]

In 2013, Mitchell J. Neubert and three colleagues at Baylor University found that entrepreneurs in the United States prayed more often than non-entrepreneurs and, moreover, that they were more likely to believe in a God that was "personally responsive to them."[59] Although most of the participants in the aforementioned study were Christians, researchers in Indonesia—a majority Muslim country—likewise found that "the practice of spirituality positively strengthens students' capacity to acquire the psychological attributes of potential entrepreneurs" and that Indonesian students with a spiritual practice and worldview were more likely to plan on becoming entrepreneurs.

Although the correlation between spirituality and entrepreneurship might differ from country to country or region to region, the Indonesian researchers point out that there are "physical and mental advantages" to a spiritual practice including "better focus," greater "self-awareness," "improved learning capacities," and "low nervousness levels."[60] To this list, we might add big-picture thinking, imagination, a sense of purpose, and self-restraint or the ability to delay satisfaction.

Executives that regularly practice meditation include Ramani Ayer, former chairman and CEO of The Hartford Financial Services Group, Steve Rubin, former CEO and chairman of United Fuels International, and Def Jam music label founder Russell Simmons. Moreover, under CEO Marc Benioff, Salesforce has integrated "mindfulness zones" into every floor of its offices for its forty thousand employees. There, employees put their smartphones into a basket out of their reach and "clear their minds." Benioff believes that this practice of mindfulness and the cultivation of the "beginner's mind" is essential to the innovation that Salesforce (which makes over $13 billion in annual revenue) relies on to succeed.[61]

CONSCIOUSNESS

SciTech Daily has said that if we are to rely upon artificial intelligence it must "be able to process information, or 'think,' like humans."[62] Certainly, to create technology that mimics human intelligence—minus any uncomfortable biases—is the aim of probably the majority of AI scientists today. However, there is a fundamental error in this conception, not merely in regard to technology but perhaps especially in regard to human beings. As we have noted with our discussion of ratio and intellectus and of hypnosis, sleep, creativity, and so on, we are not merely rational creatures. Indeed, as marketing companies have known for roughly a century (and psychoanalysts, hypnotists, and religions have known for far longer), we are motivated by desire, fear, sexual arousal, and so on, and not by cold, rational calculation. Conscious thinking or calculation is only one aspect of human consciousness and probably quite a small aspect.

Our experience of the world is aesthetic and tactile. We have instincts or "gut feelings" that sometimes save people's lives, by telling us that a particular stranger poses a threat to us, for example. We use our intuition in the practice of an art. We experience inspiration in moments of relaxation. And we switch from one state of consciousness to another throughout the day: sleep, hypnagogia, waking consciousness in which we might think rationally to solve a problem, daydreaming, a state of hypnosis or light trance, and so on.

At a certain level of mastery in a field, things seem to happen all by themselves. Charles Dickens said that his books were revealed to him and rather than inventing anything he would simply write down what he was witnessing.[63] And of course, professional dancers practice until they "transition from conscious awareness" of a technique or routine to "automatic performance" in which the body seems to move itself.[64] The same might be said of any skill requiring muscle memory.

We noted earlier that inspiration sometimes strikes when an individual is sleepy. But let's look a little more closely at dreams.

In 1797, the poet and philosopher Samuel Taylor Coleridge was living and working in a farmhouse in Somerset, England. For whatever reason, one afternoon Coleridge decided to take a few grains of opium. Subsequently, while still sitting in his chair he entered a "profound sleep" that lasted for about three hours. On awakening, he discovered that a poem had formed in his mind, as if it had been received rather than carefully worked out by him—consciously at least. The poet was soon disturbed by a visitor and, having to chit-chat about other things, forgot much of the poem. What remained was his best-known work "Kubla Khan: Or, a Vision in a Dream: A Fragment."[65]

Fashion designer Karl Lagerfeld often had ideas come to him in dreams, which he would sketch on waking up. Such inspiration was behind his spring couture collection, unveiled in January 2015. Seeing it all in a dream, Lagerfeld drew it out as precisely as possible immediately after waking up from his night's sleep.[66]

Other cultural works inspired by dreams include *Tintin in Tibet* by Hergé (Georges Prosper Remi),[67] the song "Yesterday" by Paul McCartney, and a number of paintings by artists Albrecht Durer and Salvador Dali.[68] In regard to "Yesterday," the songwriter woke up with the tune in his head, got out of bed, and started playing it on the piano. At first he "couldn't believe" that he had written it.[69]

After dreaming of a snake biting its own tail, the nineteenth-century chemist August Kekulé conceived of the ring structure of benzene, which was used to make the first synthetic dye and is widely used today in the manufacturing of plastics, synthetic fibers, and detergents.[70] Likewise, pharmacologist and psychobiologist Otto Loewi discovered the function of the neurotransmitter acetylcholine and consequently recognized that communication between nerve cells is primarily electrical rather than chemical, after dreaming of a scientific experiment, which he quickly conducted.[71]

The evolutionary purpose of dreaming has long been pondered with suggestions ranging from emotional regulation to the processing of daily experiences. Erik Hoel, a research assistant professor at Tufts' Allen Discovery Center, has suggested that by adding "noise" or complexity, dreams prevent us from becoming "overfit,"[72] or overspecialized in one specific area or with one specific task and thus neglecting to develop a general way of thinking that can be applied to different areas of life or different and perhaps unpredicted challenges. Certainly if we think about our dreams, we find that they piece together thoughts that we've had with things that we've seen or experienced over the last few days and weeks; and they piece them together in unusual and counterintuitive ways. Sometimes a dream might be disturbing. Sometimes it might be pleasant. But the fusing of different ideas and information is exactly what creators do in their waking life, for instance by introducing medieval calligraphy, "fonts," to modern technology.

We saw at the beginning of this book that increasing expertise within a specialization can lead to a steady decrease in the quality of work and that conversely the greatest figures in different fields tended to have experience in other fields. And of course, in this final chapter we have argued for the need for complexity (e.g., through connections) and creativity—the exploration of our own consciousness being part of that.

Consciousness is the awareness of complexity. Someone looking at a problem from the outside will always think that the solution is simple and obvious. The more we learn about anything, or the more conscious of it we become, the more complicated it becomes. It doesn't matter if that thing is history, design, biology, politics, relationships, or something else. What appears to be straightforward from the outside can be filled with contradictions once you get deep into it. The genius finds a simple solution sometimes by stripping something down to its essence or, more likely, introducing even more complexity by going outside of the problem or outside of their field to another seemingly unrelated field. Hence McQueen turning to fairy tales and movies for inspiration; Steve Jobs's introduction of fonts, learned of when he was studying calligraphy from a Trappist monk; or Apple's adoption of the Japanese minimalist or Zen aesthetic; and Carl Jung's adoption of myths to explain psychoanalysis. Going outside of our specialism to another field is rather like dreaming. It allows us to imagine and to see what we know more abstractly. And it enables us to think counterintuitively.

When we're conscious of complexity, we can think counterintuitively. In most corporations, meetings are a kind of Socratic dialogue between the senior members of the team that are present, with subordinates remaining largely or even entirely silent. Such meetings may be unnecessarily dragged out but they are straightforward; no one wants to contradict their manager when their livelihood partly depends on not rocking the boat.

Silent subordinates means that no one feels that their authority is being undercut. But such meetings don't allow complexity to emerge. Consequently things can get myopic with obvious flaws going unconsidered. We only have to look at the branding disasters of some giant American corporations in recent years to realize that that isn't always a good thing. In contrast, in meetings at Amazon, Jeff Bezos makes a point of speaking last and prefers to have the most junior person speak first. This enables all thoughts to be aired and complexity to emerge if more junior members introduce ideas or observations that no one else thought of, with Bezos or other senior staff able to rein things in and find the path forward.[73]

But complexity isn't just for the boardroom. While some American professionals claim that microdosing LSD helps them to feel calm or to be more social,[74] it is probable that complexity lies behind the rediscovery of psychedelics at the higher levels of American business, including in Silicon Valley. Not to be taken lightly, LSD can facilitate visionary experiences. It can bring to the fore new ideas and feelings. And it can fill the individual with a profound sense of connection and meaning.

Like LSD, dreams break through—and can disrupt—repetition. Even when they aren't providing inspiration to artists or answers to scientific problems, both dreams and psychedelic experiences often leave the experiencer with a profound sense of meaning. They can be interpreted as prophetic or as messages or visitations from a realm beyond that of material existence. Consequently, long after awakening they have made the dreamer or psychonaut think, feel, and act differently. Some people even like to talk about their dreams as if they are real-life events.

As artificial intelligence becomes increasingly able to model—or perhaps collate—human thought, so the more intelligent, creative, and outgoing members of our societies will increasingly peer into the non-rational depths of their own psyches and of the human psyche more generally. Dreams may provide answers from time to time but mostly they provide a sense of mystery and provoke in us the notion that there is something meaningful about the world or about us that lies partially hidden and that cannot be explained.

As you might have noticed, it is miserable, miserly, and angry people—people who are stuck and unadaptable—who have an answer for everything. Joyful, successful people ask questions. And despite whatever practical aims they might entertain, they have a sense of destiny or of being attracted to something beyond them. Indeed, we earlier heard CEO and economist Ram Nidumolu speaking of his experience of ancient Hindu rituals and how it affected him. AI might give us more answers, but that might make us less happy.

We will look into the nonrational also to tap our creative potential (we earlier looked at inspiration in relation to self-hypnosis) and to understand who we are and what we truly desire. We will do it for relaxation and rejuvenation and for private recreational escape from the mundane. And of course, altered states of consciousness, perhaps with the aim of having visions, will be cultivated as spiritual experiences. Overarchingly, though, we will develop our different and nonrational states of consciousness to become whole or integrated and to both embody our true nature and to be more adaptable in an ever-changing and unpredictable world.

To develop ourselves as a whole, we will need to recognize that—in contrast to AI systems—we pass through multiple states of consciousness each day: sleep, hypnagogia, daydreaming, waking consciousness, and so on. Successful individuals will learn when and how to use logical reasoning as well as nonrational processes and techniques such as meditation and hypnosis. And they will dive deep into consciousness not only to understand other people but to understand themselves and to connect to a deep sense of meaning. And, also unlike AI, at a certain level of mastery, we are capable of facing and solving complex challenges in both rational and nonrational ways: calculation, instinct, intuition, counter-intuitive thinking, inspiration, and flow.

Notes

CHAPTER I. CHAOS

1. Bauman, *Liquid Modernity*, 1–2.
2. O'Grady, *Thales of Miletus*, 59–60.
3. O'Grady, *Thales of Miletus*, 60.
4. Forman, "Of the Division of Chaos."
5. Abraham, *A Dictionary of Alchemical Imagery*, 33–34.
6. Gleick, *Chaos*, 8.
7. Gleick, *Chaos*, 3–4.
8. Gleick, *Chaos*, 69.
9. Gleick, *Chaos*, 80; May, "Simple Mathematical Models with Very Complicated Dynamics," 459–67.
10. Gleick, *Chaos*, 80.
11. Aristotle, *Politics* 1:1259a, 9; Allen, *Greek Philosophy: Thales to Aristotle*, 27.
12. Amen, *Trading Thalesians*, 9.
13. Chris Taylor, "A little honesty might preserve the family fortune," Reuters online, June 17, 2015.
14. Bandura, "The Psychology of Chance Encounters and Life Paths," 747.
15. Bandura, "The Psychology of Chance Encounters and Life Paths," 751.
16. Molly Gregory, "10 Chance Meetings That Changed the World," Mental Floss website, May 22, 2020.
17. Bandura, "The Psychology of Chance Encounters and Life Paths," 747–55.

CHAPTER 2.
CHARACTER AND CULTURE

1. Durant and Durant, *The Lessons of History*.
2. Farghal, *Jordan's Proverbs as a Window into Arab Popular Culture*, 67.
3. Genç, "An Evaluation of Ibni Khaldun's Thoughts of the Economical World," 57.
4. Milenko Martinovich, "Americans' Partisan Identities Are Stronger Than Race and Ethnicity, Stanford Scholar Finds," Stanford Report, Stanford University website, August 31, 2017; Westwood et al., "The Tie That Divides."
5. Graham M. Vaughan, "Henri Tajfel: Polish-Born British Social Psychologist," Britannica website, last updated May 7, 2024.
6. Matthew Hutson, "Why Liberals Aren't as Tolerant as They Think," Politico website, May 9, 2017.
7. Po Bronson and Ashley Merryman, "The Creativity Crisis," *Newsweek* website, July 10, 2010, updated January 23, 2014.
8. Cammaerts, *The Laughing Prophet*, 1 (paraphrasing G. K. Chesterton).
9. Jean H. Lee, "Kim Jong-il: Legendary Golfer and Mythical Powers even in Death," Associated Press, *Christian Science Monitor* website, December 22, 2011.
10. Editorial Board, "America Has a Free Speech Problem," *New York Times* website, March 18, 2022.
11. Carlo Diano, "Epicurus: Greek Philosopher," Britannica website, updated February 29, 2024; David Konstan, "Epicurus," Stanford Encyclopedia of Philosophy website, revised July 8, 2022.
12. Tim Worstall, "The Average American Today Is 90 Times Richer Than the Average Historical Human Being," *Forbes* website, January 6, 2016, updated June 29, 2021.
13. Tilly Alexander, "I tried Tesco's Easter Hot Cross Bun Range Including One That Isn't in Stores Yet and One Flavour Was Pure Heaven," My London website, March 23, 2022.
14. Keping, "The Beauty Ladder and the Mind-Heart Excursion," 35.
15. Hill, *Think and Grow Rich*, 273.
16. Hill, *Think and Grow Rich*, 274.
17. Hill, *Think and Grow Rich*, 261.
18. D'Israeli, *The Literary Character*, 146–55.

19. Simkhovitch, "Rome's Fall Reconsidered," 232–33.
20. D'Israeli, *The Literary Character*, 156–62.
21. Simonton, "Exceptional Creativity Across the Life Span"; Ellis, *A Study of British Geniuses*; McCurdy, "The Childhood Patterns of Genius," 33–38.
22. Ford, *My Philosophy of Industry*, 27.
23. Veblen, *The Theory of the Leisure Class*, 34.
24. Bellezz, Paharia, and Keian, "Conspicuous Consumption of Time," 119.
25. Pieper, *Leisure*, 78, 41.
26. Pieper, *Leisure*, 19.
27. Pieper, *Leisure*, 46.
28. Pieper, *Leisure*, 28.
29. *The Ayn Rand Lexicon*, 198.
30. Pieper, *Leisure*, 65.
31. Pieper, *Leisure*, 67.
32. Pieper, *Leisure*, 43–45.
33. Ford, *My Philosophy of Industry*, 10.
34. Dutton and Charlton, *The Genius Famine*, 1.
35. Krzewińska et al., "Ancient Genomes Suggest the Eastern Pontic-Caspian Steppe as the Source of Western Iron Age Nomads."
36. Haywood, *Great Migrations*, 30–32.
37. Haywood, *Great Migrations*, 42–43.
38. Haywood, *Great Migrations*, 100.
39. Haywood, *Great Migrations*, 106.
40. Vivian Nutton, "Galen: Greek Physician," Britannica website, updated March 6, 2024.
41. Bernd Magnus, "Friedrich Nietzsche: German Philosopher," Britannica website, updated April 23, 2024.
42. Nietzsche, *The Joyful Wisdom*, 168.
43. Michio Kaku, "Albert Einstein: German-American Physicist," Britannica website, updated April 22, 2024.
44. Marilyn McCully, "Pablo Picasso: Spanish Artist," Britannica website, updated May 20, 2024.
45. B. R. Nanda, "Mahatma Gandhi," Britannica website, updated April 23, 2024.
46. Horowitz, *Occult America*, 189–90.
47. Anusha Natarajan, Mohamad Moslimani, and Mark Hugo Lopez, "Key Facts about Recent Trends in Global Migration," Pew Research Center website, December 16, 2022.

48. Janet Alvarez, "Immigrants Outperform Native-Born Americans on Two Key Measures of Financial Success," NBC News website, June 21, 2019.
49. Peter Coy, "Why So Many Children of Immigrants Rise to the Top," *New York Times* website, July 11, 2022.
50. Partnership for a New American Economy, *The "New American Fortune" 500*, New American Economy website, June 2011, 2; Alvarez, "Immigrants Outperform Native-Born Americans on Two Key Measures of Financial Success."
51. Deniz Çam, "From Sergey Brin to Elon Musk: Meet the 43 Immigrants on the Forbes 400," *Forbes* website, updated October 4, 2018.
52. *Forbes*, "Profile: Osman Kibar Founder, CEO, Samumed," *Forbes* website, April 4, 2023.
53. Jeffrey S. Passel and D'Vera Cohn, "U.S. Unauthorized Immigrants Are More Proficient in English, More Educated Than a Decade Ago," Pew Research Center website, May 23, 2019.
54. Coy, "Why So Many Children of Immigrants Rise to the Top."
55. Dyer et al., "The Innovator's DNA."
56. Steve Jobs, "'You've Got to Find What You Love,' Jobs Says," Stanford Report website, June 12, 2005.

CHAPTER 3.
THE EIGHT LAWS OF SELF-EMPOWERMENT

1. Cook, *Practical Lessons in Hypnosis*, 37–38.
2. Duckworth, *Grit*, 8.
3. Cook, *Practical Lessons in Hypnosis*, 38.
4. Aristotle, *The Nicomachean Ethics*, 25.
5. Cook, *Practical Lessons in Hypnosis*, 41.

CHAPTER 4.
EIGHT DAILY POWER PRACTICES

1. Friedman and Diamond, *Food Sanity*, 112.
2. Cassidy et al., "Motivations and Experiences of Volunteers and Patients in Mental Health Befriending."
3. Amy Fleming, "Nutritional Psychiatry: Can You Eat Yourself Happier?," *Guardian* website, March 18, 2019.

4. Mayo Clinic Staff, "Exercise: 7 Benefits of Regular Physical Activity," Mayo Clinic website, August 26, 2023.
5. Kelly McGonigal, "Five Surprising Ways Exercise Changes Your Brain," Greater Good Magazine website, January 6, 2020.
6. Crystal Raypole, "A Simple Guide to the Endocannabinoid System," Healthline website, May 17, 2019.
7. Cheryl D. Fryar and Cynthia L. Ogden, "Prevalence of Underweight among Adults Aged 20 Years and Over: United States, 1960–1962 Through 2007–2010," National Center for Health Statistics, CDC website, last reviewed November 6, 2015.
8. Gaby Galvin, "The U.S. Obesity Rate Now Tops 40%," U.S. News website, February 27, 2020.
9. Harvard Health Publishing, "Taking Aim at Belly Fat," Harvard Health Publishing website, March 26, 2024; Galvin, "The U.S. Obesity Rate Now Tops 40%."
10. Pete Leibman, "A Fit CEO Is an Effective CEO: Why Leaders Need to Make Time for Exercise," Salon website, September 9, 2018.
11. Matthew Hoffman, "Low Testosterone and Your Health," WebMD website, April 28, 2023.
12. Claire Sissons, "Typical Testosterone Levels in Males and Females," Medical News Today website, updated March 7, 2024; Rachel Gurevich, "Why Testosterone Is Important," Very Well Health website, May 22, 2023.
13. Shippen and Fryer, *The Testosterone Syndrome*, 5.
14. Shippen and Fryer, *The Testosterone Syndrome*, 8.
15. Shippen and Fryer, *The Testosterone Syndrome*, 5.
16. Mayo Clinic Staff, "Fitness Program: 5 Steps to Get Started," Mayo Clinic website, December 5, 2023.
17. David DiSalvo, "Why Getting Too Little Sleep Could Lead to Risky Decision Making," *Forbes* website, updated September 11, 2017.
18. Laura Goldman, "6 Harmful Effects of Lack of Sleep—and Why It's Unhealthy," Business Insider website, July 7, 2020.
19. Minda Zetlin, "Getting Too Little Sleep Makes You Terrible at Your Job, according to a Clinical Psychologist," Inc. website, December 28, 2018.
20. Meilan Solly, "Nearly One-Third of Americans Sleep Fewer Than Six Hours Per Night," Smithsonian Magazine website, December 26, 2018.
21. Cleveland Clinic, "Human Growth Hormone (HGH)," Cleveland Clinic website, last reviewed June 21, 2022.

22. Neil Howe, "America the Sleep-Deprived," *Forbes* website, August 18, 2017.
23. Goldman, "6 Harmful Effects of Lack of Sleep."
24. David L. Chandler, "Study: Better Sleep Habits Lead to Better College Grades," MIT News, MIT website, October 1, 2019.
25. Kelly Cappello, "The Impact of Sleep on Learning and Memory," Chronobiology and Sleep Institute, Perelman School of Medicine website, December 21, 2020.
26. Dali, *50 Secrets of Magic Craftsmanship*, 33.
27. Dali, *50 Secrets of Magic Craftsmanship*, 34.
28. Daniel A. Cox, "The State of American Friendship: Change, Challenges, and Loss," Survey Center of American Life, American Survey Center website, June 8, 2021.
29. Jeanna Bryner, "Close Friends Less Common Today, Study Finds," LiveScience website, November 4, 2011.
30. Mehl et al., "Eavesdropping on Happiness"; Jenn Granneman, "Why We Need to Have Deeper Conversations," *Psychology Today* website, June 17, 2017.
31. SINC, "Our Brains Synchronize During a Conversation," Science Daily website, July 20, 2017; Pérez et al., "Brain-to-Brain Entrainment."
32. Nicklas Balboa and Richard D. Glaser, "The Neuroscience of Conversations," *Psychology Today* website, May 16, 2019.
33. Mayo Clinic Staff, "Positive Thinking: Stop Negative Self-Talk to Reduce Stress," Mayo Clinic website, November 21, 2023.
34. Horowitz, *The Power of the Master Mind*, 18.
35. Andrew Perrin, "Slightly Fewer Americans Are Reading Print Books, New Survey Finds," Pew Research Center website, October 19, 2015.
36. Carmine Gallo, "Bill Gates and Other Billionaires Say This 1 Habit Is the Secret to Their Success," Inc. website, December 7, 2017.
37. Gallo, "Bill Gates and Other Billionaires Say This 1 Habit Is the Secret to Their Success."
38. Carmelites of Australia and Timor-Leste, "Lectio Divina," Carmelites website, accessed December 30, 2024.
39. Nidumolu, *Two Birds in a Tree*, 47.
40. Nidumolu, *Two Birds in a Tree*, 51.
41. Nidumolu, *Two Birds in a Tree*, 52.
42. Nidumolu, *Two Birds in a Tree*, 8, 17.
43. Stein et al., "A Sacred Commitment."

44. Monfort et al., "The Impact of Anticipating Positive Events on Responses to Stress."
45. Gao et al., "The Neural Basis of Delayed Gratification."
46. Chinta and Andersen, "Dopaminergic Neurons."
47. Chokroverty and Billiard, *Sleep Medicine*, 17.
48. Nutton, *Ancient Medicine*, 104, 111.
49. Londino, *Tiger Woods*, 5.
50. Martin Domin, "Teenage Sparring, Hypnotism and Two Crushing Defeats: Frank Bruno's Heavyweight Rivalry with Mike Tyson," *Mirror* website, February 26, 2021.
51. Cashmore, *Sport Psychology*, 133; Johnson, "Hypnotist Held Key to Ken Norton's Win," 45–46.
52. *Richard Bandler's Guide to Trance-formation*, 2.
53. Tator and Latson, *More Time for You*, 79.
54. Keri Wiginton, "What Happens to Your Body When You Relax," WebMD website, last reviewed August 29, 2024.
55. Anastasia Stephens, "Relax Your Way to Perfect Health," *Independent* website, July 28, 2009.
56. Sue McGreevey, "Relaxation Response Proves Positive," *Harvard Gazette* website, October 13, 2015; Stahl et al., "Correction: Relaxation Response and Resiliency Training and Its Effect on Healthcare Resource Utilization."
57. Shelley, *Frankenstein*, x.
58. Dali, *50 Secrets of Magic Craftsmanship*, 38–41.
59. Dali, *50 Secrets of Magic Craftsmanship*, 44.

CHAPTER 5.
THE LANGUAGE OF ENCHANTMENT

1. Angela Wintle, "Gerald Ratner: 'I Spent Seven Years in Bed after That Speech,'" *Telegraph* website, July 4, 2021.
2. Cassirer, *The Myth of the State*, 282–83.
3. Cassirer, *The Myth of the State*, 283.
4. Fisher III et al., "Reflections on the Hope Poster Case."
5. Simon Jeffery, "Edwards: Hope Is on Its Way," *Guardian* website, July 29, 2004; Martin Sieff, "Edwards' Message: 'Hope Is on the Way,'" UPI website, July 29, 2004.

6. Associated Press, "Clinton: 'I'm in, and I'm in to Win,'" NBC News website, January 20, 2007.
7. Ben Smith, "Undecided: Hillary Keeps Shifting Slogans," Politico website, January 3, 2008; Matthew Continetti, "Mixed Metaphor Alert," *Washington Examiner* website, November 12, 2007.
8. Moine and Lloyd, *Unlimited Selling Power*, 15.
9. Moine and Lloyd, *Unlimited Selling Power*, 72–74.

CHAPTER 6. SELF-TALK

1. Horowitz, *One Simple Idea*, 148.
2. Horowitz, *One Simple Idea*, 147.
3. Coué, *Self-Mastery Through Conscious Autosuggestion*, 14.
4. Coué, *Self-Mastery Through Conscious Autosuggestion*, 21–22.
5. *Richard Bandler's Guide to Trance-formation*, 26–28.
6. Coué, *Self-Mastery Through Conscious Autosuggestion*, 21.
7. Sull and Spinosa, "Promise-Based Management."

CHAPTER 7.
FIVE ROOTS OF PERSONAL PRESENCE

1. DeNova Research, "Impact of Botox Treatment into the Upper One Third of the Face an Area on Mood and Self-Appearance Satisfaction," Clinical Trials NCT04439825, National Library of Medicine, Reagan-Udall Foundation website, March 15, 2023.
2. Ronnberg and Martin, *The Book of Symbols*, 392–94.
3. Pearsall et al., "Changes in Heart Transplant Recipients That Parallel the Personalities of Their Donors."
4. Pearsall et al., "Changes in Heart Transplant Recipients," 194.
5. Pearsall et al., "Changes in Heart Transplant Recipients," 198.
6. Spiegelman, *Reich, Jung, Regardie & Me*, 12.
7. Charles Q. Choi, "Why Women Prefer 'Chill' Guys," NBC News website, September 14, 2010; Ananya Mandal, "Calm Men Preferred by Women," News Medical website, September 16, 2010.
8. *Musashi's Book of Five Rings*, 28.
9. Nair et al., "Do Slumped and Upright Postures Affect Stress Responses?"

CHAPTER 8. CHAOS REVISITED: STRANGENESS AND AUTHORITY

1. Cook, *Practical Lessons in Hypnosis*, 27.
2. O'Hanlon, *A Guide to Trance Land*, xii.
3. O'Hanlon, *A Guide to Trance Land*, xiii.
4. Sutherland, *Alchemy*, vii.
5. Moine and Lloyd, *Unlimited Selling Power*, 61.
6. Godin, *Purple Cow*, 3.
7. Rogers, *Diffusion of Innovations*, 22.
8. Rogers, *Diffusion of Innovations*, 284.
9. Isaac Crowson, "Stranger Sex: Half of Brits Enjoy Fantasising about Strangers When Making Love to Partner, Study Shows," *U.S. Sun* website, November 21, 2022; Ian Kerner, "Top 5 Female Sex Fantasies . . . and What They Mean," *Huffington Post* website, July 11, 2011.
10. Caroline McGuire, "Are You Sexier Overseas? Travellers Reveal the Countries Where They Are Considered Far More Attractive Than at Home," *Daily Mail* website, November 8, 2016; Hana Hong, "75 Percent of People Think This One Trait Makes You More Attractive," *Reader's Digest* website, October 4, 2022.
11. Jessica Orwig, "Scientists Have Discovered How Common Different Sexual Fantasies Are," Business Insider website, October 31, 2014.
12. Megan Logan, "Science Says You Should Take Your Dates to Horror Movies," Inverse website, October 27, 2016; Debra Kelly, "What Happens to Your Body When You Watch a Scary Movie," Grunge website, updated February 22, 2023.

CHAPTER 9. THE SIX CS: A SURVIVAL GUIDE FOR A TIME OF AI

1. Abigail Johnson Hess, "Former Stanford Admissions Officer: Colleges Aren't Looking for Well-Rounded Students," CNBC website, updated February 4, 2018.
2. Steven Greenhouse, "We Must Start Preparing the US Workforce for the Effects of AI," *Guardian* website, February 29, 2024.
3. Lauren Leffer, "Humans Absorb Bias from AI—and Keep It after They Stop Using the Algorithm," *Scientific American* website, October 26, 2023.

4. Cade Metz, "In Two Moves, AlphaGo and Lee Sedol Redefined the Future," Wired website, March 16, 2016.
5. Tony T. Wang, Adam Gleave, Tom Tseng et al., "Adversarial Policies Beat Superhuman Go AIs," Cornell University, arXiv website, July 13, 2023.
6. Ryuichiro Hataya, Han Bao, and Hiromi Arai, "Will Large-Scale Generative Models Corrupt Future Datasets?" Cornell University, arXiv website, November 15, 2022.
7. Guo et al., "The Curious Decline of Linguistic Diversity: Training Language Models on Synthetic Text," Cornell University, arXiv website, November 16, 2023.
8. Viviane Callier, "A Massive LinkedIn Study Reveals Who Actually Helps You Get That Job," *Scientific American* website, September 16, 2022; Rajkumar et al., "A Causal Test of the Strength of Weak Ties."
9. Data Freaks, "How Social Networks Can Keep the Poor Down and the Rich Up," *Forbes* website, updated March 23, 2015.
10. Thomas C. Corley, "I Spent 5 Years Studying Rich People, and I Can Tell You They're Laser-Focused on Building the Type of Relationships Anyone Can Seek," Business Insider website, December 3, 2019.
11. "Life of Jacqueline B. Kennedy," Kennedy Presidential Library and Museum website, accessed January 2, 2025.
12. Esposito, *Dinner in Camelot*, 38.
13. Samsung Newsroom, "Samsung's San Jose Headquarters Amenities Help Ease Commute for Employees," Samsung website, May 1, 2017.
14. Waber et al., "Workspaces That Move People."
15. Gleick, *Chaos*, 90.
16. Gleick, *Chaos*, 86.
17. Rachel Lebowitz, "9 Artists Who Are Scientific Innovators—from Leonardo da Vinci to Samuel Morse," Artsy website, February 20, 2018.
18. Millar, "Painting with Light and Space: Antoni de Lenval Malinowski."
19. Tamer, "On the Chopping Block, Again."
20. Po Bronson and Ashley Merryman, "The Creativity Crisis," *Newsweek* website, July 10, 2010, updated January 23, 2014.
21. Bronson and Merryman, "The Creativity Crisis."
22. Sutherland, *Alchemy*, 83.
23. Bly, *The Copywriter's Handbook*, 64–66.
24. Zumdahl et al., *Chemistry*, 36.

25. Paul McCartney, "Paul McCartney Tries to Recapture a Fresh Sound," interview by Steve Inskeep, NPR website, October 20, 2005.
26. Seth Godin, "The Coordinators," Seth's Blog website, January 28, 2021.
27. McCormack, *What They Don't Teach You at Harvard Business School*, xii–xiii
28. Caroline McClatchey and Alex Murray, "Fashion Week: Why Does Central Saint Martins Produce So Many Designers?" BBC website, September 16, 2011; IDP: International Education Specialists, "Fashion Design Courses in United Kingdom," IDP website, accessed January 2, 2025.
29. James Anderson, "23 Things You Need to Know about Studying Fashion at Central Saint Martins," i-D website, March 9, 2019.
30. Kabir Chibber, "The New School," *T: The New York Times Style Magazine* website, April 14, 2011.
31. McClatchey and Murray, "Fashion Week."
32. Johnny Davis, "The Fashion Stars of Central Saint Martins," *Observer* website, February 6, 2010.
33. Errika Gerakiti, "The Majestic Art of Alexander McQueen," Daily Art Magazine website, August 20, 2024.
34. Davis, "The Fashion Stars of Central Saint Martins."
35. Allen, "The Real Costs of Bad Management."
36. Angela Davis, Susan Davis, and Carly Quarst, "The Cost of a Bad Boss," MPR News website, October 18, 2021.
37. Betsy Mikel, "1 Personality Trait Steve Jobs Always Looked for When Hiring for Apple," Inc. website, December 11, 2017.
38. Simonton, "Creative Development as Acquired Expertise."
39. Bryan Hood, "The World's Most Expensive Burger Has Wagyu Beef, Beluga Caviar—and Costs $6,000," Robb Report website, July 5, 2021.
40. Angela Giuffrida, "How the Return of Traditional Skills Is Boosting Italy's Economy," *Guardian* website, April 1, 2017.
41. Praachi Raniwala, "Indian Craftsmanship Was the Focus of Dior's Fall 2023 Show," *Harper's Bazaar* website, April 3, 2023.
42. Don-Alvin Adegeest, "Hermès, Investing in the Future of Its Craftsmanship, to Open Two Leathergoods Workshops," FashionUnited website, March 16, 2022; Spencer, Mimosa, "Hermès Opens New Leather Goods Workshop in France," WWD, April 6, 2018; Hermès, "Hermès Vintage," Avvenice website, March 24, 2024.
43. Bethanie Ryder, "Hermès' Entry into the Metaverse Hails a New Era for Digital Luxury Fashion," Jing Daily website, September 9, 2022.

44. Bill Chappell, "Americans Do Not Walk the Walk, and That's a Growing Problem," NPR website, April 16, 2012.
45. Jeffrey Kluger, "How Telling Stories Makes Us Human," *Time* website, December 5, 2017; UCL News, "Storytellers Promoted Co-operation among Hunter-Gatherers Before Advent of Religion," UCL website, December 5, 2017.
46. Michael Glover, "The Big Question: How Many of the Paintings in Our Public Museums Are Fakes?" *Independent* website, April 16, 2010.
47. University of Bonn, "Why Expensive Wine Appears to Taste Better: It's the Price Tag," Science Daily website, August 14, 2017.
48. Sutherland, *Alchemy*, 215.
49. Pencavel, "The Productivity of Working Hours"; Kabir Sehgal and Deepak Chopra, "Stanford Professor: Working This Many Hours a Week Is Basically Pointless. Here's How to Get More Done—By Doing Less," CNBC website, updated March 21, 2019.
50. Marguerite Ward, "3 Science-Backed Reasons Having a Hobby Will Help Your Career," CNBC website, August 2, 2017.
51. Dyer et al., "The Innovator's DNA."
52. Aristotle, *Nichomachean Ethics*, 1139b15.
53. Kevin McLaughlin, "14 Tech Execs Who Could Probably Kick Your Butt in a Fight," Business Insider website, June 15, 2013.
54. Jen Murphy, "A CEO's Straight Line from Martial Arts to Leadership," *Wall Street Journal* website, June 3, 2017.
55. James Burton, "Exercise Soothes the Savage Boss," NIU Today website, January 25, 2012.
56. Laura Entis, "Marathon Runners Make Better CEOs, Study Finds," NBC News website, September 12, 2014.
57. Max Nisen, "9 Famous Execs Who Majored in Philosophy," Business Insider website, January 19, 2014.
58. Jackson and Delehanty, *Sacred Hoops*, 5.
59. Neubert, "Entrepreneurs Feel Closer to God Than the Rest of Us Do."
60. Hadi et al., "Should Spirituality Be Included in Entrepreneurship Education Program Curriculum to Boost Students' Entrepreneurial Intention?"
61. Catherine Clifford, "Salesforce CEO Marc Benioff: Why We Have 'Mindfulness Zones' Where Employees Put Away Phones, Clear Their Minds," CNBC website, November 5, 2019.
62. University of Glasgow, "Developing Artificial Intelligence That 'Thinks' Like Humans," SciTech Daily website, October 18, 2021.

63. Martin Weaver, "Hearing Voices Allowed Charles Dickens to Create Extraordinary Fictional Worlds," *Guardian* website, August 23, 2014.
64. Diane Solway, "How the Body (and Mind) Learns a Dance," *New York Times* website, May 28, 2007.
65. Hargraves, *Dreaming Big*, 9.
66. Kaiser, *Karl Lagerfeld*, 241.
67. Peeters, *Hergé*, 275–78.
68. Ribeiro, *The Oracle of Night*, 218.
69. Ribeiro, *The Oracle of Night*, 218.
70. Robinson, "Chemistry's Visual Origins"; Rocke, *Image and Reality*, 293.
71. McCoy and Tan, "Otto Loewi (1873–1961)."
72. Taylor McNeil, "A New Theory for Why We Dream," Tufts Now website, February 18, 2021.
73. Jef Haden, "Why Jeff Bezos Always Speaks Last (and So Should You), Backed by Social Science," Inc. website, December 18, 2023.
74. Hannah Kuchler, "How Silicon Valley Rediscovered LSD," Financial Times website, August 10, 2017.

Bibliography

Abraham, Lyndy. *A Dictionary of Alchemical Imagery*. Cambridge University Press, 1998.

Allen, Mark. "The Real Costs of Bad Management—and What You Can Do about It." *Graziadio Business Review* 22, no. 1 (2019).

Allen, Reginald E., ed. *Greek Philosophy: Thales to Aristotle*. Free Press, 1991.

Amen, Saeed. *Trading Thalesians: What the Ancient World Can Teach Us about Trading Today*. Palgrave Macmillan, 2014.

Aristotle. *The Nicomachean Ethics*. Translated by David Ross. Oxford University Press, 2009.

Aristotle. *Politics*. Translated by H. Rackham. Harvard University Press, 1932.

Bandler, Richard. *Richard Bandler's Guide to Trance-formation: How to Harness the Power of Hypnosis to Ignite Effortless and Lasting Change*. Health Communications, 2008.

Bandler, Richard, and John Grinder. *The Structure of Magic: A Book about Language and Therapy*. Science and Behavior Books, 1975.

Bandura, Albert. "The Psychology of Chance Encounters and Life Paths." *American Psychologist* 37, no. 7 (1982): 747–55.

Bauman, Zygmunt. *Liquid Modernity*. Polity, 2000.

Bellezz, Silvia, Neeru Paharia, and Anat Keian. "Conspicuous Consumption of Time: When Busyness and Lack of Leisure Time Become a Status Symbol." *Journal of Consumer Research* 44 (June 2017): 118–38.

Bly, Robert W. *The Copywriter's Handbook: A Step-By-Step Guide to Writing Copy That Sells*. St. Martin's Griffin, 2005.

Cammaerts, Emile. *The Laughing Prophet: The Seven Virtues and G. K. Chesterton.* ACS Books, 1937.

Caronia, Lisa M., Andrew A. Dwyer, Douglas Hayden, Francesca Amati, Nelly Pitteloud, and Frances J. Hayes. "Abrupt Decrease in Serum Testosterone Levels after an Oral Glucose Load in Men: Implications for Screening for Hypogonadism." *Clinical Endocrinology* 78 (2013): 291–96.

Cashmore, Ellis. *Sport Psychology: The Key Concepts.* Routledge, 2002.

Cassidy, Megan, Rose Thompson, Rawda El-Nagib, Lauren M. Hickling, and Stefan Priebe. "Motivations and Experiences of Volunteers and Patients in Mental Health Befriending: A Thematic Analysis." *BMC Psychiatry* 19, no. 116 (2019).

Cassirer, Ernst. *The Myth of the State.* Yale University Press, 1978.

Chinta, Shankar J, and Julie K. Andersen. "Dopaminergic Neurons." *International Journal of Biochemistry Cell Biology* 37, no. 5 (2005): 942–46.

Chokroverty, Sudhansu, and Michel Billiard, eds. *Sleep Medicine: A Comprehensive Guide to Its Development, Clinical Milestones, and Advances in Treatment.* Springer, 2015.

Cook, William Wesley. *Practical Lessons in Hypnosis.* Thompson & Thomas, 1901.

Coué, Émile. *Self-Mastery Through Conscious Autosuggestion.* George Allen & Unwin, 1984.

Dali, Salvador. *50 Secrets of Magic Craftsmanship.* Must Have Books, 2021.

D'Israeli, Isaac. *The Literary Character, or The History of Men of Genius.* London: Henry Colburn, 1828.

Duckworth, Angela. *Grit: The Power of Passion and Perseverance.* Scribner, 2016.

Durant, Will, and Ariel Durant. *The Lessons of History.* Simon & Schuster Paperbacks, 1996.

Dutton, Edward, and Bruce G. Charlton. *The Genius Famine: Why We Need Geniuses, Why They're Dying Out, Why We Must Rescue Them.* University of Buckingham Press, 2015.

Dyer, H., Hal Gregersen, and Clayton M. Christense. "The Innovator's DNA." *Harvard Business Review*, December 2009.

Ellis, H. *A Study of British Geniuses.* Rev. ed. Houghton Mifflin, 1926.

Esposito, Joseph A. *Dinner in Camelot: The Night America's Greatest Scientists, Writers, and Scholars Partied at the Kennedy Whitehouse.* ForeEdge, 2018.

Farghal, Mohammed. *Jordan's Proverbs as a Window into Arab Popular Culture: The Fox in the Blackberries.* Cambridge Scholars, 2019.

Fisher III, William W., Frank Cost, Shepard Fairey et al. "Reflections on the Hope Poster Case." *Harvard Journal of Law & Technology* 25, no. 2 (Spring 2012): 244–338.

Ford, Henry. *My Philosophy of Industry.* George G. Harrap, 1929.

Forman, Simon. "Of the Division of Chaos." MS Ashmole 240, n.d. Bodleian Library, Oxford.

Friedman, David, and Harvey Diamond. *Food Sanity: How to Eat in a World of Fads and Fiction.* Turner Publishing, 2018.

Gao, Zilong, Hanqing Wang, Chen Lu et al. "The Neural Basis of Delayed Gratification." *Science Advances* 7, no. 49 (2021): eabg6611.

Gleick, James. *Chaos: Making a New Science.* Viking, 1987.

Godin, Seth. *Purple Cow: Transform Your Business Through Being Remarkable.* Portfolio, 2003.

Hadi, Sutarto, Ersis Warmansyah Abbas, and Ismi Rajiani. "Should Spirituality Be Included in Entrepreneurship Education Program Curriculum to Boost Students' Entrepreneurial Intention?" *Frontiers in Education* 7 (2022).

Hargraves, Matthew. *Dreaming Big: Sleep and the Practice of Drawing.* Drawing Institute, Morgan Library & Museum, 2021.

Haywood, John. *The Great Migrations: From the Earliest Humans to the Age of Globalization.* Quercus, 2008.

Hill, Napoleon. *Think and Grow Rich.* Sound Wisdom, 2017.

Horowitz, Mitch. *Occult America: The Secret History of How Mysticism Shaped Our Nation.* Bantam Books, 2009.

———. *One Simple Idea: How Positive Thinking Reshaped Modern Life.* Crown Publishers, 2014.

———. *The Power of the Master Mind.* Gildan Media, 2019.

Jacka, Felice N., Adrienne O'Neil, Rachelle Opie et al. "A Randomised Controlled Trial of Dietary Improvement for Adults with Major Depression (the 'SMILES' Trial)." *BMC Medicine* 15, no. 1 (2017): 23.

Jackson, Phil, and Hugh Delehanty. *Sacred Hoops: Spiritual Lessons of a Hardwood Warrior.* Hachette Go, 2020.

Johnson, John H., ed. "Hypnotist Held Key to Ken Norton's Win." *Jet* 44, no. 4 (April 19, 1973): 45–46.

Kaiser, Alfons. *Karl Lagerfeld: A Life in Fashion.* Translated by Isabel Adey. Cernunnus, 2022.

Keping, Wang. "The Beauty Ladder and the Mind-Heart Excursion: Plato and Zhuangzi." In *Cultivating a Good Life in Early Chinese and Ancient Greek Philosophy: Perspectives and Reverberations*, edited by Karyn Lai, Rick Benitez, and Hyun Jin Kim. Bloomsbury Academic, 2019.

Krzewińska, Maja, Gülşah Merve Kılınç, Anna Juras et al. "Ancient Genomes Suggest the Eastern Pontic-Caspian Steppe as the Source of Western Iron Age Nomads." *Science Advances* 4, no. 10 (2018): eaat4457.

Londino, Lawrence. *Tiger Woods: A Biography*. Greenwood Press, 2005.

May, Robert M. "Simple Mathematical Models with Very Complicated Dynamics." *Nature* 261 (June 1976): 459–67.

McCormack, Mark H. *What They Don't Teach You at Harvard Business School*. Profile Books, 2014.

McCoy, Alli N., and Yong Siang Tan. "Otto Loewi (1873–1961): Dreamer and Nobel Laureate." *Singapore Medical Journal* 55, no. 1 (2014): 3–4.

McCurdy, Harold G. "The Childhood Patterns of Genius." *Horizon* Magazine, 1960, first published at *Journal of the Elisha Mitchell Scientific Society* 73, pt. 2 (1957): 448–62.

Mehl, Matthias R., Simine Vazire, Shannon E. Holleran, and C. Shelby Clark. "Eavesdropping on Happiness: Well-being Is Related to Having Less Small Talk and More Substantive Conversations." *Psychological Science* 21, no. 4 (2010): 539–41.

Millar, Angel. "Painting with Light and Space: Antoni de Lenval Malinowski." *OPEN* Magazine, 2023.

Moine, Donald, and Kenneth Lloyd. *Unlimited Selling Power: How to Master Hypnotic Selling Skills*. Prentice Hall, 1990.

Monfort, Samuel S., Hannah E. Stroup, and Christian E. Waugh. "The Impact of Anticipating Positive Events on Responses to Stress." *Journal of Experimental Social Psychology* 58 (2015): 11–22.

Musashi, Miyamoto. *Musashi's Book of Five Rings: The Definitive Interpretation of Miyamoto Musashi's Classic Book of Strategy*. Translated by Stephen F. Kaufman. Tuttle, 1994.

Nair, Shwetha, Mark Sagar, John Sollers III, Nathan Consedine, and Elizabeth Broadbent. "Do Slumped and Upright Postures Affect Stress Responses? A Randomized Trial." *Health Psychology* 34, no. 6 (2015): 632–41.

Neubert, Mitchell J. "Entrepreneurs Feel Closer to God Than the Rest of Us Do." *Harvard Business Review*, October 2013.

Nidumolu, Ram. *Two Birds in a Tree: Timeless Indian Wisdom for Business Leaders.* Beret-Koehler, 2013.

Nietzsche, Friedrich. *The Joyful Wisdom (La Gaya Scienza).* Translated by Thomas Common. T. N. Foulis, 1910.

Nutton, Vivian. *Ancient Medicine.* 2nd ed. Routledge, 2013.

O'Grady, Patricia F. *Thales of Miletus: The Beginnings of Western Science and Philosophy.* Routledge, 2016.

O'Hanlon, Bill. *A Guide to Trance Land: A Practical Handbook of Ericksonian and Solution-Oriented Hypnosis.* W. W. Norton, 2009.

Pascal, Blaise. *Pascal's Pensees.* E. P. Dutton, 1958.

Pearsall, Paul, Gary E. R. Schwartz, and Linda G. S. Russek. "Changes in Heart Transplant Recipients That Parallel the Personalities of Their Donors." *Journal of Near-Death Studies* 20, no. 3 (Spring 2002): 191–206.

Peeters, Benoît. *Hergé: Son of Tintin.* Translated by Tina Kover. John Hopkins University Press, 2012.

Pencavel, John, "The Productivity of Working Hours." Institute of Labor Economics, Discussion Paper Series, No 8129. IZA website, April 2014.

Pérez, Alejandro, Manuel Carreiras, and Jon Andoni Duñabeitia. "Brain-to-Brain Entrainment: EEG Interbrain Synchronization While Speaking and Listening." *Scientific Reports* 7, no. 4190 (2017).

Pieper, Josef. *Leisure: The Basis of Culture; The Philosophical Act.* Translated by Alexander Dru. Ignatius Press, 2009.

Rajkumar, Karthik, Guillaume Saint-Jacques, Iavor Bojinov et al. "A Causal Test of the Strength of Weak Ties." *Science* 377, no. 6612 (September 15, 2022): 1304–10.

Rand, Ayn. *The Ayn Rand Lexicon: Objectivism from A to Z.* Edited by Harry Binswanger. Penguin, 1988.

Ribeiro, Sidarta. *The Oracle of Night: The History and Science of Dreams.* Translated by Daniel Hahn. Pantheon Books, 2021.

Robinson, Andrew. "Chemistry's Visual Origins." *Nature* 465 (May 2010): 36.

Shelley, Mary W. *Frankenstein: Or, the Modern Prometheus.* London: Henry Colbourn and Richard Bentley, 1831.

Rocke, Alan J. *Image and Reality: Kekulé, Kopp, and the Scientific Imagination.* University of Chicago Press, 2010.

Rogers, Everett M. *Diffusion of Innovations.* 5th ed. Free Press, 2003.

Ronnberg, Ami, and Kathleen Martin, eds. *The Book of Symbols: Reflections on Archetypal Images.* Taschen, 2010.

Shippen, Eugene, and William Fryer. *The Testosterone Syndrome: The Critical Factor for Energy, Health, and Sexuality—Reversing the Male Menopause.* M. Evans, 1998.

Simkhovitch, Vladimir Gregorievitch. "Rome's Fall Reconsidered." *Political Science Quarterly* 31, no. 2 (June 1916): 201–43.

Simonton, Dean Keith. "Creative Development as Acquired Expertise: Theoretical Issues and an Empirical Test." *Developmental Review* 20, no. 2 (2000): 283–318.

———. "Exceptional Creativity Across the Life Span: The Emergence and Manifestation of Creative Genius." *International Handbook on Innovation* (2003): 293–308.

Spiegelman, J. Marvin. *Reich, Jung, Regardie & Me: The Unhealed Healer.* New Falcon, 2009.

Stahl, James E., Michelle L. Dossett, A. Scott LaJoie et al. "Correction: Relaxation Response and Resiliency Training and Its Effect on Healthcare Resource Utilization." *PLoS One* 12, no. 2 (2017): e0172874.

Stein, Daniel H., Nicholas M. Hobson, and Juliana Schroeder. "A Sacred Commitment: How Rituals Promote Group Survival." *Current Opinion in Psychology* 40 (2021): 114–20.

Sull, Donald, and Charles Spinosa. "Promise-Based Management: The Essence of Execution." *Harvard Business Review*, April 2007.

Sutherland, Rory. *Alchemy: The Dark Art and Curious Science of Creating Magic in Brands, Business, and Life.* William Morrow, 2019.

Tamer, Mary. "On The Chopping Block, Again." *Harvard Ed. Magazine*, Summer 2009.

Tator, Rosemary, and Alesia Latson. *More Time for You: A Powerful System to Organize Your Work and Get Things Done.* Amacom (American Management Association), 2011.

Veblen, Thorstein. *The Theory of the Leisure Class.* Oxford University Press, 2007.

Waber, Ben, Jennifer Magnolfi, and Greg Lindsay. "Workspaces That Move People." *Harvard Business Review*, October 2014.

Westwood, Sean J., Shanto Iyengar, Stefaan Walgrave, Rafael Leonisio, Luis Miller, and Oliver Strijbis. "The Tie That Divides: Cross-National Evidence of the Primacy of Partyism." *European Journal of Political Research* 57, no. 2 (2018): 333–54.

Yanek, Lisa R., Brian G. Kral, Taryn F. Moy et al. "Effect of Positive Well-Being on Incidence of Symptomatic Coronary Artery Disease." *American Journal of Cardiology* 112, no. 8 (October 15, 2013): 1120–25.

Yılmaz Genç, Sema. "An Evaluation of Ibni Khaldun's Thoughts of the Economical World." In *Globalisation Dimension & Impacts: Global Studies Series*, vol. 2, edited by Hilal Yıldız, Ismail Siriner, and Farhang Morady. IJOPEC Publication, 2015.

Zumdahl, Steven S., Susan A. Zumdahl, and Donald J. DeCoste. *Chemistry: An Atoms First Approach*. Cengage Learning, 2016.

Index

abstinence, 25–27
acquaintances, and friendships, 8
adopters, types of, 109
agnomination, defined, 79–80
Agra tribe, 139–40
AI, 116–20, 136, 138
   and consciousness, 148, 152–53
   flaws of, 118–20, 144
al-Afghani, Jamal ad-Din, 32
alchemy, 5
Alexander the Great, 31
Amazon, 152
anticipation, 24–25
apprenticeships, 135
Aquinas, Thomas, 28
Arab peoples, 31
Archimedes, 143–44
Aristotle, 6, 81, 144
arrogant people, have answers, 17
art, 129–30, 140
artistic people, 123–24
asabiyyah, 12, 106
asceticism, 22–25, 24
asclepieion, 66
Asclepius, 66

atheism, 20–21
attractiveness, 65
Aurelius, Marcus, 19
authority, 105–115
   defined, 105
authority and strangeness, 105–15
   in society, 108–15
autosuggestions, 84–85
Ayer, Ramani, 148

balance, meaning of, 25
Bandler, Richard, 66
Bandura, Albert, 8–9
Bauman, Zygmunt, 4
beauty, seeing, 64
befriending, 51
Being-centered leadership, 60
belief, 10, 46
   and changing your life trajectory, 22
   in God, 20–22
Benioff, Marc, 148
Besant, Annie, 33
Bezos, Jeff, 152
Birnbaum, Scott, 122
Blavatsky, Mme., 33, 110–11

Bly, Robert (copywriter), 126
Bly, Robert (poet), 99
Botox, 94
boundaries, 40–41
brain, controlled by food, 50
brands, 77, 106
   and authority, 109
breath, the
   breathing exercise, 100
   and emotional states, 99–100
   and personal presence, 99
Buddha, depictions of, 95
buisness education, 130
bunbu-ryodo, 145
Butterfield, Stewart, 146
butterfly effect, 6
buzzwords, 76

Cajal, Santiago Ramón, 123
calm exterior, and personal presence, 100–102
calmness, 100–102
   attraction to calm men, 101–2
Cammaerts, Emile, 20
Cassatt, Mary, 127
Cassirer, Ernst, 73–74
celebrities, as authority, 109–10
celibacy, 25–27
Central Saint Martins College of Art and Design, 129–32
   characteristics of studying at, 130–32
Chalayan, Hussein, 131
changing times, responses to, 1, 4, 136
chaos, 84–90
   and AI, 116
   awaits the unprepared, 83

defined, 2
freedom and, 47–48
life as, 5
study of, 5–6
character, 144–48
   and craft, 135
   and culture, 10–36
   and our ability to navigate, 9
   vs. personality, 89
   and wisdom, 145
characteristics of human beings, listed (nine), 11
charismatic people, and presence, 91
Charlie Foxtrot, 75
childhood experiences, as foundation for our life, 8
Chinese culture, 145
   three teachings, 141
"chin up," 103
Christensen, Clayton M., 35
Christianity, decline of, 12
Christmas, 61
Clinton, Hillary, 80
clothing, 39, 103
Cochran, Johnny, 80–81
Coleridge, Samuel Taylor, 149
collateral damage, 75
commanding oneself, 42
competence, and our ability to navigate, 9
complaining, 57, 90
complexity, 151–52
concentration of thought, and self-empowerment, 44
confident people, 17
conformity, 109
connection, 121–24, 151

consciousness, 148–53
  and complexity, 151
  switching from one state to another, 149
consumerism, 23, 28
contemplation, 64–65
  takeaway related to, 64–65
conversation, deep, 56–57
  takeaway related to, 57
Cook, William Wesley, 38–48, 106, 110
cooking, 63
  learning to cook, 51–52
Corbusier, Le, 123
corporations, changes in, 1
cortisol, study of, 101–2
Coué, Émile, 66, 84–85, 87
courage, 43–44
CQ (creative quotient), 125
craft, 132–33
  and character, 135
creative people, crossing disciplines, 122–24
creativity, 15–18, 125–32
  and curiosity, 17–18
  and daring, 128
  suspicion of, 15
creators, as disruptors, 13
criminals, 111–12
culture, 122, 138–44
  cultural comparing, 36
  defined, 27, 138
curiosity, cultivating, 17–18

Dali, Salvador, 55–56, 69, 70, 123, 124, 150
Darwin, Charles, 26
dating, 24
decadence, defined, 23
Degas, Edgar, 127
deletions, 85–86
determination, 41
  and self-empowerment, 41–42
Dickens, Charles, 149
diet, 49, 50–52
  diet study, 50–51
  takeaway related to, 51–52
Dior, 135
D'Israeli, Isaac, 26
distortions, 85–86
divergence test, 126
divergence thinking, 126–27
dreams, 149–52
Duckworth, Angela, 41
Durant, Ariel, 10
Durant, Will, 10
Dyer, Jeffrey, 35

early adopters, 109
Ed (teenager treated by Erickson), 107
education systems, 58, 116–17, 125, 130, 145
Eid Al-Fitr, 61
eight daily power practices, 49–71
  listed, 50
Eight Laws of Self-Empowerment, the, 38–48
  listed, 38
Einstein, Albert, 32
emotions, freezing the, 101
enchantment, language of, 72–83
endocannabinoid system, 52
English people, emergence of the, 31

epicureanism/asceticism, 22–25
    meaning of "epicurean," 22–23
    takeaway related to, 25
Epicurus, 22–23
Erickson, Milton, 66, 106–8
estrogen, 53
exaggerations, 87
excuses, not to act, 46

face, the. *See also* facial expressions
    allowing it to relax, 96–97
    face exercise, 96–97
    and personal presence, 92–97
    tension in the, 97
facial expressions
    and mindset, 96
    our default facial mask, 93
failure, 47
    not a reason to quit, 41
fake paintings, 140
family unit, 10–11
    in various societies, 14–15
fantasy, and relationships, 113–14
fashion, is everywhere, 130
fat, 52–53
fearlessness, 43–44
festivals, 61–62
fight-or-flight response, 80
fitness, 52–54
five roots of personal presence, 91–104
    listed, 92
fluids, 4
food, 50, 63
Ford, Henry, 27–30
Forman, Simon, 5
fragmentation, 142

Frankenstein (Shelley), 68–69
Franklin, Benjamin, 32
French Impressionists, 128
Freud, Sigmund, 66
Friedman, David, 50
friends/friendships, 56, 63
    and our character and gravitas, 8

Galen, 31–32
game face, 94–95
Gandhi, Mahatma, 33
Gates, Bill, 57
generalizations, 76, 85–86
generals, 139
genius, 26–27, 30
global village, 12
Go (game), 118
God, belief in, 10, 20–22, 46
Godin, Seth, 108, 130
"God is dead," 32
"Golden Boy" burger, 134
good, the, 24–25
"go with the flow," 4
Granovetter, Mark, 121
Greek culture, 60–61
group loyalty/individualism, 12–14
    takeaway related to, 14
growth, as incremental, 42
Guigo, 58
Gurdjieff, G. I., 64, 111

Hall, Manly P., 111
Harvest Festival, 61
health, 49.
    recommendations, ix
    and self-empowerment, 39–40

heart, the
　associated with power, 98
　heart exercise, 99
　and personal presence, 98–99
heart transplants, 98
Hergé, 150
Hermès, 135–36
Hill, Napoleon, 25–26
hobbies, 143
Hockney, David, 124
Ho Kepos, 23
holistic, defined, 91
honesty, 83
hope, as magic word, 77–78
hormones, 53
horror movies, 114–15
hospitality, 18
Hudson, Liam, 125–26
human beings
　nine characteristics described, 11–36
　nine characteristics listed, 11
　six traits listed, 10
human growth hormone, 54
hypnagogia, 67
hypnosis, 65–71, 105
　and clients' use of language, 82
　and hypnotist's physique, 106
　and meditation, 66–67
　origins of, 65–66
　and positive use of language, 83
　qualities of a successful hypnotist, 38
　and strangeness and authority, 105

ibn Talib, 'Ali, 19
icons, 77
identifying with others, 14

immigrants, 31–36
　and cultural comparing, 36
　living with risk, 35
　psychological pressures on, 34–35
　success of, 34
individualism, and group loyalty, 12–14
influence, operates reciprocally, 9
innovation/tradition, 14–18
　takeaway related to, 17–18
innovators, 109
　and manageable risks, 16–17
inspiration, 143–44, 149
　and self-hypnosis, 68–69
instincts, 149
intellectus, 29, 64, 145, 147
internet, development of the, 119
inventiveness, and knowledge, 126
IQ, 125–26

Jacka, Felice, 50
Jackson, Phil, 147
Jesus, depictions of, 95
jewelry store, 72–73
Joan of Arc, 19
Jobs, Steve, 8–9, 127, 133, 137, 151
Jung, Carl, 5, 66, 151

kaloi k'agathoi, 25
KataGo, 118
Kennedy, Jacqueline, 122
Kennedy, John F., 122
Khaldun, Ibn, 12
Kim Jong Il, 20
Kim Jong Un, 20
Krishna, depictions of, 95
"Kubla Khan," 149

Lagerfeld, Karl, 150
laggards (late adopters), 109
landscapes, and portraits, 94, 138–39
language
  contemplating its magic, 89–90
  deceptive, 75–76
  magic and, 73–77
  shapes perception, 87
leadership, 60
  and promises, 88–89
  as self-awareness, 3
lectio divina, 58
leisure, and work, 27–30
Levin, Gerald, 146
life
  as chaos, 5
  as liquid, 5
liquid modernity, 4
logic, kills magic, 107
loyalty, 12–14
LSD, 152

magic
  killed by logic, 107
  and language, 73–77
"make America great again," 80
male menopause, 53
Malinowski, Antoni De Lenval, 123–24
Mandelbrot, Benoit, 123, 143
Mandelbrot set, 123
manifesting, 45–46
Mascagni, Pietro, 134
Mastermind sessions, 57
May, Robert M., 6
McCartney, Paul, 128, 150
McCartney, Stella, 124

McCormack, Mark H., 130
McQueen, Alexander, 119, 132–33, 137, 143, 151
meditation, 148
  and posture, 103–4
mental aspect of life, 146–47
Merks-Benjaminsen, Joris, 146
Migliano, Andrea, 139
migration/settlement, 11, 31–36
  takeaway related to, 36
mindfulness, 148
minimizations, 86–87
missionary, 110–11
mistakes, and creativity, 127–28
Monet, Claude, 127
Montbron, 135–36
"moral majority," new, 13
motivating individuals, 14
Musashi, Miyamoto, 19, 102
Musk, Elon, 57

Nara, Yoshitomo, 124
nation-state
  decline of belief in, 12
  unification within, 141
negative mindset, 67
-ness suffix, 74–75
Neubert, Mitchell J., 147
neuro-linguistic programming, 108
New Thought, 45–46, 71
Newton, Isaac, on chaos, 5–6
Nidumolu, Ram, 59–60, 62, 153
Nietzsche, Friedrich, 32
Nin-in, 21–22
"no," saying, 40
nonlinear systems, 6

Nowruz, 61
nutrients, need for, 52–53

Obama, Barack, 77
obi, defined, 103
olive presses, 6–7
openness to experience, 14
opportunity, awaits the prepared, 83
Oughton, Diana, 8
overweight, 52–53
overwriting, of old beliefs, 87

paintings, fake, 140
pencil, benefits of a, 126–27
perception, and self-empowerment, 48
personality
   vs. character, 89
   five-factor model, 14
personal presence, five roots of, 91–104
philokalia, 24
Phoenicians, 31
physical training, 49, 52–54, 63, 146
   benefits of, 52–53
   takeaway related to, 53–54
Picasso, Pablo, 26, 32, 123
Pieper, Josef, 28–29
Plato, 145
Plucker, Jonathan, 125
pneuma, defined, 99
police interview, 78–79, 111
portraits, and landscapes, 94, 138–39
positive thinking, 45–46, 71
Post-It Notes, 127
posture, 102–4
   and character, 102–3
   and clothing, 103
   and meditation, 103–4
   and mood, 103
   and personal presence, 102–4
   posture exercise, 104
   and self-empowerment, 40
power
   possessing, 40
   and relaxation, 100
power practices, eight daily, 49–71
   listed, 50
prana, defined, 99
prayer, 147–48
prejudice, 12–14
presence, defined, 91
progress, 77
   belief in, 15
promises, 88–89
psychedelics, 152
Ptah, 98
public face, 96

Quakers, 24

Rand, Ayn, 29
random encounters, branching power of, 8–9
ratio, 29, 64, 144–45, 147
Ratner, Gerald, 72–73
Razzle Dazzle, 129
react, vs. respond, 89
reading, deep, 57–59
   takeaway related to, 59
receptivity, and self-assertion, 18–19
Reich, Wilhelm, 101
relationships
   and authority and strangeness, 113–14
   that drain time, 27

relaxation, 30, 68
  exercise of relaxing the body, 99
  exercise of relaxing the face, 96–97
  self-hypnosis and, 68
relaxation-response techniques, 68
religious faith/secularism, 20–22
  takeaway related to, 22
repetition, of words, 82
resilience, 41
respond, vs. react, 89
rhetoric, 81
rigid responsiveness, 101
ritual, 59–64
  death rituals, 59–60
  purpose of, 60–62
  takeaway related to, 63–64
robbery, attempted robbery of the author, 111–13
Roman Empire, and sexuality, 26–27
romantic relationships, 113–14
Roosevelt, Franklin D., 139
Roque, Jacqueline, 26

Samsung headquarters, 122
Saturnalia, 61
saving face, 95
science, vs. alchemy, 5–6
secularism, and religious faith, 20–22
self, sense of, 14
self-assertion, appropriate, 19
self-assertion/receptivity, 18–19
  takeaway related to, 19
self-awareness, and self-possession, 45
self-confidence, and self-empowerment, 40–41

self-development, 19
Self-Empowerment, Eight Laws of, 38–48
self-hypnosis, 65–71, 84–85
  reasons for, 67–68
  and relaxation, 68
  takeaway related to, 70–71
self-possession, and self-empowerment, 45–48
self-talk, 84–90
serendipity, 122
settlement, and migration, 31–36
sex, 25–27
  and genius, 26–27
sex/abstinence, 25–27
  takeaway related to, 27
sexual relationships, 113–14
Shelley, Mary W., 68–69
Silver, Spencer F., 127
Six Arts, 145
six C's, 116–53. *See also* character; connection; consciousness; craft; creativity; culture
  listed, 121
skill, and craft, 133–34
skills, traditional, 135
sleep, 54–56
  and inspiration, 68–69
  lack of, 54–55
  and learning, 55
  takeaway related to, 56
SMILE study, 50–51
Smith, Daniel, 139
smoking, 84–85
societies, and unification and fragmentation, 141–42
Socrates, 4–5

Index

spiritual aspect of life, 147–48, 153
   and success, 147
Stoker, Bram, 26
storytelling, 139–40
strangeness
   and arousal, 114–15
   and authority, 105–15
   defined, 105
stress, the face of, 96
strong ties, 121–22
success, 25–26, 46–47, 153
   as dependent on relationships, 83
   and IQ and CQ, 125
   and spiritual aspect of life, 147
Sufism, as way of the heart, 98
Sutherland, Rory, 107, 141

Tajfel, Henri, 13
tea, pouring tea story, 21–22
testosterone, 53
Thales of Miletus, 4
   olive presses bought by, 6–7
"the only thing we have to fear," 139
Theosophical Society, the, 33
Thiel, Peter, 146
thinking, 137
   and AI, 148–49
   in the education system, 58
Thoth, 73
thought, 66–67
   concentration of, 44
trading, Thales and, 7
tradition, and innovation, 14–18
traditional crafts, and luxury brands, 135
traits of human beings, listed, 10, 11
Trump, Donald, 80

ummah, 18
unacceptable feelings, 101
uncertainty, prevalences of, 1–3
upright, defined, 103

vaping, 84–85
Veblen, Thorstein, 28
virtues, five, 144
Vishnu, 99
vision, 41, 45
visualization, and self-hypnosis, 70
Vivekananda, Swami, 111

walking, 65, 136–37
warrior-monk, 18–19
water
   as primal substance, 4
   sipping, 63–64
we (use of term), 81
weak ties, 121–22
wealth, 7–8
   in the world, 23
what you want, clarity about, 19
whole, defined, 91
wine, expensive, 141
wisdom, and character, 145
words, magic words, 73–77, 81–82
work
   focusing on, 41
   working long hours, 142–43
work/leisure, 27–30
   takeaway related to, 30
   working long hours, 142–43
Wozniak, Steve, 8–9
writing, the act of, 119–20

Zen, pouring tea story, 21–22